ITALIAN
C·O·O·K·I·N·G

GOLDEN APPLE PUBLISHERS

Cover picture published by permission of THORN EMI
Major Electrical Appliances Limited from *Microwave
Baking* by Val Collins, published in the United
Kingdom by David and Charles Limited.

ITALIAN COOKING

A GOLDEN APPLE PUBLICATION/
PUBLISHED BY ARRANGEMENT WITH OTTENHEIMER PUBLISHERS INC.

JUNE 1986

GOLDEN APPLE IS A TRADEMARK OF GOLDEN APPLE PUBLISHERS

ISBN 0-553-19859-9
Printed in Korea

Contents

Appetizers

Asparagus with Mayonnaise Sauce

1	**(10-ounce) package frozen asparagus spears, partially thawed**
1	**tablespoon butter, melted**
1	**tablespoon dry sherry**
2	**teaspoons onion, finely minced**
¼	**teaspoon salt**
	Dash pepper

Mayonnaise Sauce
1	**egg**
1	**teaspoon dry mustard**
1	**teaspoon salt**
	Dash cayenne pepper
1	**cup olive oil**
3	**tablespoons lemon juice**
	Bibb lettuce
	Parsley
	Paprika

Place asparagus in small casserole, separating spears. Mix butter, sherry, and seasonings. Pour over asparagus; cover. Bake at 350°F 25 minutes, until crisp-tender. Cool; refrigerate.

In blender container, combine egg, seasonings, and 1/4 cup oil. Cover; blend thoroughly. Remove center portion of blender cover. With blender running, add 1/2 cup oil in small steady stream. Slowly add lemon juice. Add remaining 1/4 cup of oil in thin steady stream. Blend until thick and smooth. Scrape mayonnaise down from sides of blender occasionally.

Arrange asparagus on beds of Bibb lettuce; coat with mayonnaise. Garnish with parsley and paprika. Serve as first course. Makes 4 servings.

Mozzarella Cheese Sandwiches with Anchovy Sauce

Anchovy Sauce
¼ cup butter
2 anchovy fillets
1 tablespoon capers, drained and chopped
2 tablespoons parsley, chopped
Juice of ½ lemon

Mozzarella Cheese Sandwiches
16 thin slices Italian bread (½ inch thick)
8 thick slices mozzarella cheese (⅜ inch thick)
3 eggs
Salt to taste
½ cup dry bread crumbs
¼ cup butter or margarine

Melt butter in small skillet; do not brown. Rinse anchovies under cold running water; chop finely. Add with capers and parsley to butter. Add lemon juice; stir well. Keep sauce warm.

Remove crusts from bread. Lay 1 cheese slice between 2 bread slices; press together. In a small bowl, beat eggs and a pinch of salt. Dip sandwiches into egg; dredge in bread crumbs. Heat butter over moderate heat in a heavy skillet. Add cheese sandwiches. Cook until golden brown on one side; turn and cook on other side. Serve immediately topped with anchovy sauce. Makes 4 servings.

Stuffed Artichokes

4 medium globe artichokes
¾ cup dry bread crumbs
3 tablespoons Parmesan cheese, grated
1 tablespoon parsley, chopped
½ teaspoon garlic salt
¼ teaspoon dried oregano, crumbled
¼ teaspoon pepper
2 tablespoons butter
2 tablespoons olive oil
1 cup boiling water

Remove stems from artichokes. Cut about 1/2 inch from tips of leaves, using kitchen shears. Drop into boiling salted water; cook 5 minutes. Drain; shake to remove water; cool.

Combine bread crumbs, cheese, parsley, garlic salt, oregano, and pepper. Mix well.

Tap bases of artichokes on a flat surface to spread the leaves. Stuff each artichoke with 1/4 of bread-crumb mixture; spoon it between the leaves. Put artichokes into a saucepan or stove-top casserole; place them close together so they do not tip over. Top each artichoke with 1/2 tablespoon butter and 1/2 tablespoon oil. Pour in boiling water and cover. Cook over low heat 35 to 45 minutes or until artichokes are tender. Makes 4 servings.

Clams Casino

2	**dozen cherrystone clams**
2	**tablespoons olive oil**
1	**tablespoon butter**
½	**cup onion, finely minced**
¼	**cup green pepper, finely chopped**
2	**cloves garlic, peeled and chopped**
1	**cup dry bread crumbs**

4	**slices crisp bacon, crumbled**
½	**teaspoon dried oregano, crumbled**
2	**tablespoons Parmesan cheese, grated**
	Parsley flakes and paprika
	Olive oil

Wash and scrub clams well to remove grit. Place on a baking sheet. Put into 450°F oven until shells open. Remove meat from shells; chop. Reserve chopped clams; discard 1/2 of shells.

Heat 2 tablespoons oil and the butter in a small skillet. Add onion, pepper, and garlic; sauté until tender. Remove from heat; cool. Add bread crumbs, bacon, oregano, cheese, and reserved clams; mix well. Fill clam shells with mixture. Sprinkle with parsley flakes and paprika. Drizzle with olive oil. Bake in 450°F oven until lightly browned (about 7 minutes). Serve hot. Makes 6 servings.

Italian Vegetable Dip

½	**cup olive oil**
½	**cup butter**
4	**cloves garlic, peeled and finely minced**
1	**(2-ounce) can anchovies, drained and finely chopped**
	Freshly ground pepper

10	**to 12 cups assorted raw vegetables, peeled, trimmed and cut-up: cherry tomatoes, green peppers, celery, carrots, mushrooms, cauliflower, radishes, and zucchini**
1	**loaf crusty Italian bread, cut into slices**

Heat olive oil and butter together over low heat in a fondue pot or a ceramic bagna cauda pot (or heat in a skillet and pour into a casserole with a candle warmer). Heat gently so that butter does not brown. Add garlic and anchovies and continue to cook until anchovies dissolve and mixture is bubbly. Reduce heat so that the mixture stays warm but does not brown and serve with the vegetables and bread.

Provide your guests with forks so that they can spear the vegetables, swirl in the sauce, and eat holding the bread like a napkin under the vegetables to collect the drippings. Makes 6 servings.

Marinated Clams

Marinated Clams

2	**pounds clam meats**
2	**onions, minced**
2	**cloves garlic, crushed**
⅓	**cup olive oil**

About ⅓ cup parsley, chopped

2	**tablespoons lemon juice**
½	**teaspoon salt**
1	**teaspoon pepper**

Garnish

1	**small head of lettuce**
2 to 3 hard-cooked eggs, cut in	**wedges**
2 to 3 tomatoes	

Sprigs of dill

Drain the clam meats well and place in a bowl. Mix the onions, garlic, oil, parsley, lemon juice, salt, and pepper and pour over the clams. Refrigerate for 2 to 3 hours.

Rinse the lettuce. Tear the larger leaves in half and place on a large plate. Place the marinated clams with most of the marinade on the lettuce. Place wedges of eggs and tomatoes around the clams. Decorate with sprigs of dill. Makes 8 to 10 servings.

Eggs Stuffed with Tuna

6 **hard-cooked eggs, peeled**	1 **tablespoon mayonnaise**
1 **(4-ounce) can oil-packed tuna, drained**	½ **teaspoon garlic powder**
1 **tablespoon parsley, minced**	¼ **teaspoon pepper, freshly ground**
½ **tablespoon capers, finely chopped**	**Parsley**
	Pimiento slivers

Cut eggs in half lengthwise and remove yolks. Put yolks in a small bowl and mash with a fork. Drain and finely chop tuna. Add to the egg yolks along with parsley, capers, mayonnaise, garlic powder, and pepper. Mix very well and stuff egg whites with yolk and tuna mixture and garnish with parsley and pimiento. Chill well. Makes 6 servings.

Marinated Garbanzo Beans

2 **(16-ounce) cans garbanzo (ceci) beans**	½ **teaspoon dried oregano, crumbled**
½ **teaspoon salt**	¼ **cup olive oil**
¼ **teaspoon pepper, freshly ground**	**Finely chopped parsley**

Drain garbanzo beans well. Place in a serving dish. Add salt, pepper, oregano and oil and stir well. Garnish with parsley and refrigerate several hours before serving. Makes 6 servings.

Note: White beans (cannelli beans) or kidney beans can be substituted for the garbanzo beans. One 4-ounce can of drained, oil-packed tuna may also be added if cannelli beans are used. Hard-cooked eggs, peeled and sliced, and quartered tomatoes would make a tasty garnish.

Melon with Prosciutto

½ **of a large ripe honeydew or cantaloupe**	**A pepper mill**
¼ **pound prosciutto**	**Lemon or lime slices**

Remove seeds and rind from the melon and slice into crescents. Cut ham slices in half and wrap a piece of ham around each piece of melon. Arrange on a platter and grind fresh pepper over ham and melon just before serving. Garnish with lemon or lime wedges. Makes 4 to 6 servings, depending on the number of other appetizers.

Note: Fresh ripe figs or papaya may be substituted for the melon.

Melon with Prosciutto

Stuffed Mushrooms

1	pound medium or large mushrooms
1	cup dry bread crumbs
2	tablespoons dried parsley flakes
2	tablespoons Parmesan cheese, grated
¼	teaspoon garlic powder
Salt and pepper	
5	tablespoons olive oil, divided

Sauce
1	small onion, chopped
2	teaspoons olive oil
1	(8-ounce) can tomato sauce
½	teaspoon sugar
¼	teaspoon oregano, crumbled
¼	teaspoon garlic powder
Salt and pepper	

Wash mushrooms well and remove stems. Hollow out mushroom caps slightly by scraping with a teaspoon. Drain well and pat dry. Combine bread crumbs, parsley, Parmesan cheese, garlic powder, salt, pepper, and 2 table-spoons of olive oil and mix well. Fill the mushrooms with the crumb mixture. Pour 3 tablespoons of olive oil in the bottom of a shallow baking dish. Tilt to coat the dish evenly. Place the mushroom caps in the oiled baking dish.

Next prepare the sauce. Sauté the onion in the oil in a small pan until tender. Add the remaining ingredients, stir well, and simmer 10 minutes. Pour the sauce evenly over the mushrooms. Bake at 350°F for 30 minutes. Makes 4 servings.

Stuffed Olives

1	(6-ounce) can jumbo pitted black olives
1	(2-ounce) can anchovy fillets
2	tablespoons olive oil
1	clove garlic, minced

2	tablespoons parsley, finely chopped
12	cherry tomatoes, stemmed
½	medium green pepper, thinly sliced

Drain olives. Drain anchovy fillets and cut each one in half. Stuff each olive with 1/2 of an anchovy fillet. Place in a serving bowl. Combine olive oil, garlic, and parsley and pour over the olives. Mix well. Chill several hours. Bring to room temperature before serving.

Garnish with cherry tomatoes and green peppers. Makes 6 servings.

Soups and Salads

Bean Soup

2	cups dried white beans	1	carrot, peeled and chopped
8	cups water	4	tomatoes, peeled and
1	teaspoon salt		coarsely chopped
6	tablespoons olive oil	1	teaspoon dried rosemary,
1	large onion, chopped		crumbled
½	cup bacon, diced	1	teaspoon sweet basil,
2	cloves garlic, peeled and		crumbled
	minced	1½ cups short pasta, cooked	
1	stalk celery, chopped	Salt and pepper	
		Parmesan cheese, grated	

Wash beans; pick over. Place in kettle with water; soak overnight. Add 1 teaspoon salt to beans; simmer until soft. With slotted spoon, remove 1/2 beans; force through sieve or food mill. Add puree to remaining beans and liquid.

Heat oil in heavy skillet. Add onion, bacon, garlic, celery, and carrots. Sauté until onion is golden. Add onion mixture, tomatoes, and seasonings to beans; cook 30 minutes. Add pasta; salt and pepper to taste. Cook 10 minutes. Serve with grated Parmesan cheese. Makes 6 servings.

Clam Soup

2 dozen cherrystone clams in shells	4 cups ripe tomatoes, peeled and coarsely chopped
3 tablespoons olive oil	¼ cup white wine
2 cloves garlic, peeled and minced	4 tablespoons Italian flat-leaf parsley, chopped

Scrub clams well under cold running water. Soak 30 minutes in cold water to cover.

Heat oil in large saucepan. Add garlic; sauté 1 minute. Add tomatoes and wine; bring to boil. Reduce heat to low; simmer 15 minutes. Keep warm.

In large frying pan or Dutch oven with close-fitting lid, bring 1 cup water to boil. Drain clams well; place in pan. Cover; steam 5 to 10 minutes, until clams open. (Discard any clams that will not open.) Place clams in shells in warm soup bowls. Strain clam broth through cheesecloth; add to tomato sauce. Mix well and pour over clams in bowls. Sprinkle with parsley and serve with garlic toast. Makes 4 servings.

Red Fish Soup

1 onion, chopped	1 bay leaf
1 green pepper, chopped	½ teaspoon salt
¼ cup celeriac (celery root), finely shredded	⅛ teaspoon black pepper
1 large clove garlic, crushed	⅔ cup dry white wine
2 tablespoons oil	⅔ pound fillets or cod, cut into pieces
2 cans crushed tomatoes	12 clams with shells
1 tablespoon tomato paste	¼ pound shelled raw shrimp
½ teaspoon basil, crumbled	Snipped parsley for garnish

Sauté onion, green pepper, celeriac, and garlic in oil over low heat for 5 minutes. Add tomatoes and tomato paste. Stir in the seasonings. Let tomato mixture simmer covered over low heat for about 30 minutes. Stir occasionally.

Add wine, fish, and clams and simmer slowly for 7 minutes. Add shrimp; simmer for another 5 minutes. Sprinkle with parsley and serve soup piping hot with a coarse bread. Makes 4 servings.

Note: The soup can be made even more elegantly if halibut, salmon, and/or lobster are added; all according to taste and pocketbook.

Pavian Soup

3	tablespoons olive oil
1	clove garlic, peeled
4	slices crusty Italian bread, 1½ inches thick

2	(13-ounce) cans regular-strength chicken broth (4 cups homemade chicken stock can be substituted)
4	eggs
4	tablespoons Parmesan cheese, freshly grated

Heat oil in small, heavy skillet. Add garlic; saute until browned. Discard garlic. Add bread slices to skillet; sauté until golden, turning once. Remove from pan; drain on paper towels.

Heat chicken broth to boiling in medium saucepan. Break eggs into bowl or saucer; slide 1 by 1 into hot broth. Poach eggs over low heat until white is set. Remove with slotted spoon; keep warm. Strain broth, heat to boiling.

Place 1 slice toasted bread in each soup plate. Top each bread slice with poached egg. Pour hot broth over egg and toast. Sprinkle each bowl with 1 tablespoon Parmesan. Serve immediately. Makes 4 servings.

Sicilian Sausage Soup

¼ **pound sweet Italian sausage (with casing removed)**	1 **(13¾-ounce) can regular strength chicken broth**
½ **cup onion, finely chopped**	½ **teaspoon dried sweet basil, crumbled**
¼ **cup carrots, peeled and chopped**	¼ **cup orzo (rice-shaped macaroni for soup, also called "soupettes")**
¼ **cup celery, chopped**	**Salt and pepper**
2 **tablespoons parsley, chopped**	
1 **(16-ounce) can Italian-style peeled tomatoes, broken up with a fork**	

In medium skillet, brown sausage; break it into small pieces as it cooks. Remove from skillet with a slotted spoon. Place into a large saucepan. Sauté onion in sausage drippings until tender. Remove onion with slotted spoon; add to sausage. Add vegetables, chicken broth, and basil to sausage mixture. Bring soup to boil; stir well. Cook over moderate heat 15 minutes.

Stir in orzo and salt and pepper to taste. Reduce heat to low; simmer covered 20 minutes or until orzo is tender. Makes 4 servings.

Green Soup with Meatballs

½ **pound fresh spinach or beet greens**	¼ **cup Parmesan cheese, grated**
½ **cup water**	1 **egg, well beaten**
¼ **teaspoon salt**	½ **cup parsley, finely chopped**
Soup	**Salt**
¾ **pound lean ground beef**	**White pepper**
½ **cup dry bread crumbs**	4 **cups beef broth**

Remove the stems from spinach and rinse well. In medium saucepan, heat water and salt. Add spinach, reduce heat to low, and cook for 3 minutes. Drain well and coarsely chop.

In a bowl, combine the ground beef, bread crumbs, Parmesan cheese, egg, parsley, salt, and pepper. Mix well and form into walnut-sized meatballs. In large saucepan, heat beef broth to boiling. Add spinach and meatballs and bring to boil again. Reduce heat to low, cover, simmer 15 minutes, and serve. Makes 4 servings.

Neapolitan Minestrone

Neapolitan Minestrone

1½ pounds beef shanks	6 cups water
1 onion, quartered	1 celery root, cleaned and cut into thin sticks
1 package soup greens (or 2 celery stalks, 1 carrot, 1 potato, 1 turnip, and a sprig of parsley, all cleaned and chopped)	¼ pound ham, cut into thin strips
	2 ounces penne or elbow macaroni
1 small bay leaf	3 tablespoons tomato paste
2 whole peppercorns	1 teaspoon dry chervil
1 clove	4 tablespoons Parmesan cheese, grated
1½ teaspoons salt	

In large Dutch oven, combine beef shanks, onion, soup greens, bay leaf, peppercorns, clove, and salt. Add water and bring to boil. Skim any foam. Reduce heat to low; simmer covered 1-1/2 to 2 hours. Remove meat and cool. Strain broth; skim fat. Return broth to pot. Dice meat from beef shanks.

Boil macaroni until tender in boiling salted water; drain. Bring broth to boil. Combine tomato paste with 1 cup broth; stir until dissolved. Add to broth in pot, along with celery root, diced beef, and ham. Cover; cook 15 minutes. Add macaroni and chervil; heat through. Sprinkle with Parmesan cheese and serve. Makes 6 servings.

Quick Mussel Soup

1 onion, chopped	20 fresh mussels, or 1 large can
1 leek, finely sliced	
1 celery stalk, finely chopped	Liquid from the mussels
2 tablespoons butter	1¼ cups white wine
3 cloves garlic, crushed	2 cups fish broth
1 teaspoon sage and salt mixture	1 tablespoon butter
	1 tablespoon flour
⅓ cup snipped parsley	⅔ pound salmon

Brown onion, leek, and celery in butter in a pot; then add garlic, sage mixture, and parsley. Dilute with mussel juice, wine, and broth, and bring to a boil.

Remove from heat and make a ball from an equal amount of butter and flour. Add this in small bits to soup and stir until it becomes smooth. Heat soup again. Add mussels and pieces of salmon, and serve immediately. Makes 4 servings.

Quick Mussel Soup

Split Pea Soup

2 cups split peas	1½ cups tomato sauce
Water	1 teaspoon sugar
1 large onion, finely chopped (about 1½ cups)	Salt and pepper
	1 bay leaf
1 clove garlic, peeled and minced	1 cup uncooked small shell macaroni
1 ounce salt pork, chopped	Romano cheese, grated
3 tablespoons olive oil	

Pick over split peas and rinse well. Place in a small bowl and cover with water. Soak overnight.

In a large saucepan, sauté onion, garlic, and salt pork in the olive oil until the onion is tender. Add soaked peas, water to cover peas, tomato sauce, sugar, salt, pepper, and bay leaf. Simmer, covered, over low heat 1-1/2 to 2 hours or until peas are tender. Remove bay leaf and add macaroni and additional water if soup is too thick. Cover and simmer for 20 minutes.

Serve hot, sprinkled with grated Romano cheese. Makes 4 to 5 servings.

Roman-Style Vegetable Soup

½ cup salt pork, finely chopped	1 quart beef broth
1 large onion, peeled and diced	1 (16-ounce) can red kidney beans, drained
1 clove garlic	1 teaspoon dried sweet basil, crumbled
3 carrots, peeled and diced	Salt and pepper
2 stalks celery, sliced	1½ cups uncooked wide egg noodles
1 parsnip, peeled and diced	Parmesan cheese, grated
½ bunch parsley, chopped	
2 large tomatoes, chopped	

Render salt pork in large pan over moderate heat. Add onion and garlic; cook until tender. Add carrots, celery, parsnip, parsley, and tomatoes; stir well. Add beef broth, beans, basil, salt, and pepper. Bring to boil; reduce heat to low. Cover; cook 1 hour. Add noodles; simmer 15 minutes, until noodles are tender.

Serve sprinkled with Parmesan cheese. Makes 4 generous servings.

Avocado Salad with Bacon

Avocado Salad with Bacon

1 pound bacon	*Dressing*
3 to 4 ripe avocados	5 tablespoons oil
4 tender stalks celery	2 tablespoons tarragon vinegar
A piece of leek	1 clove garlic, crushed
3 to 4 hard-cooked eggs	2 teaspoons light French mustard
2 tomatoes, cut in wedges	1 to 2 teaspoons Italian salad spices, or 1 teaspoon herb salt

Fry bacon in a dry pan until crisp. Place bacon on a paper towel so that fat drains off. Divide avocados in half and remove pits. Peel the halves and cut them into slices.

Alternate sliced avocado, celery, leek, bacon, egg slices, and tomato wedges in a salad bowl.

Mix dressing ingredients together and adjust the seasonings. Shake up the dressing and pour it over the salad. Makes 4 servings.

Green Salad with Croutons

Croutons
1 clove garlic, peeled and sliced
1 cup stale Italian bread, with the crust removed (save for bread crumbs), cubed
2 tablespoons olive oil

Salad
1 medium head iceberg lettuce

1 medium head romaine lettuce or endive
¼ cup Parmesan cheese, grated

Dressing
½ cup olive oil
¼ cup red wine vinegar
½ teaspoon dried oregano, crumbled
½ teaspoon salt
¼ teaspoon pepper

First, prepare croutons. Heat olive oil in a small skillet and sauté the garlic in oil over moderate heat until lightly browned. Remove garlic with slotted spoon and discard. Add bread cubes and sauté, stirring frequently, until golden brown. Drain on paper towels.

Combine dressing ingredients in a bottle or screw-top jar and shake well. Allow to stand at room temperature. Clean lettuce and pat dry. Tear into bite-size pieces and place in a salad bowl. Refrigerate until serving time.

To serve, sprinkle salad with cheese and croutons. Shake dressing well and pour over salad. Toss well and serve immediately. Makes 4 to 6 servings.

Green Salad with Croutons

Cauliflower Salad

1	small head cauliflower
¼	cup red pepper or pimiento, chopped
2	tablespoons fresh parsley (Italian flat leaf if available), chopped

¼	cup black olives, sliced
1	tablespoon capers, chopped
1	tablespoon wine vinegar
3	tablespoons olive oil
½	teaspoon dried oregano, crumbled

Wash the cauliflower, clean it, and separate into flowerettes. Slice flowerettes into thick slices. Cook in boiling salted water until crisp, but tender. Drain well. Gently mix the cauliflower, pepper, parsley, olives, and capers in a serving bowl.

Combine the wine vinegar, olive oil, and oregano and mix well. Pour over the salad and refrigerate 1 hour before serving. This salad may be garnished with anchovies if you wish. Makes 4 servings.

Tomato Salad with Basil Dressing

Dressing
½ cup olive oil
3 tablespoons red wine vinegar
1 teaspoon dried sweet basil, crumbled
½ teaspoon garlic salt
Freshly ground pepper

Salad
1 head romaine lettuce
3 medium tomatoes, peeled and thickly sliced
1 medium onion, peeled and sliced
1 (8-ounce) ball mozzarella cheese

Combine dressing ingredients in a screw-top jar or bottle and shake well. Clean the romaine and place on a serving platter. Arrange overlapping slices of tomato, mozzarella, and onion on the platter. Refrigerate until serving time. Then, shake dressing well. Pour over salad. Serve immediately. Makes 4 servings.

Macaroni Salad

1⅔ cups macaroni
4 tablespoons oil
1½ tablespoons vinegar
½ teaspoon salt
1 teaspoon thyme
¼ pound smoked sausage, cubed

About 1 cup cheese, cubed
½ cucumber, cubed
Part of 1 leek, shredded
Tomatoes
Lettuce

Boil macaroni according to directions on package. Combine oil, vinegar, salt, and thyme. Pour dressing over the hot macaroni. Let cool.

Mix sausage, cheese, cucumber, and leek with the cold macaroni. Season. Serve with tomatoes and lettuce. Makes 4 servings.

Pepper and Tomato Salad

2 medium green peppers
3 medium firm ripe tomatoes
½ cup olive oil
2 tablespoons red wine vinegar

½ teaspoon dried sweet basil, crumbled
1 tablespoon dehydrated parsley flakes
Salt and pepper, to taste

Clean green peppers and cut in thin lengthwise slices. Core tomatoes and cut into thin slices. Arrange in a serving dish. Combine olive oil, vinegar, and seasoning and mix well. Pour over the vegetables and refrigerate several hours before serving. Makes 4 servings.

Macaroni Salad

Mixed Seafood Salad

2	dozen mussels	
2	dozen small clams	
3	tablespoons olive oil	
2	pounds small squid	
½	cup white wine	
1¼	pounds medium shrimp	

Dressing

4	tablespoons olive oil
2	tablespoons lemon juice
1	teaspoon Dijon mustard
Salt	
Freshly ground pepper	

Scrub mussels and clams well under cold running water. Heat oil in large skillet with tight-fitting lid. Add mussels and clams; cover. Cook over medium-high heat, shaking pan occasionally, until shellfish open (approximately 10 minutes). Remove clams and mussels from shells; cool. Reserve juices; strain through sieve.

Wash squid; remove tentacles. Remove head, chitinous pen, and viscera; wash mantle well.

In large saucepan, combine wine and reserved juices from shellfish. Bring to boil over moderate heat. Add squid body and tentacles; cover. Simmer 10 minutes. Add shrimp; cook 15 minutes. (Squid should be tender and shrimp cooked through and pink.) Drain well. Shell shrimp; slice squid body into thin rings.

In large bowl, combine clams, mussels, squid, and shrimp.

Combine dressing ingredients. Pour dressing over seafood; mix well. Sprinkle with parsley; marinate in refrigerator 2 hours. Serve on beds of lettuce; garnish with lemon wedges. Makes 4 servings.

Rice and Chicken Salad

1	cup rice, cooked al dente (firm to the bite)
1	teaspoon Dijon mustard
½	teaspoon salt
2	teaspoons red wine vinegar
6	tablespoons olive oil
½	cup Swiss cheese, finely diced
¼	cup black olives, pitted and diced
2	tablespoons green olives, pitted and diced
¼	cup sweet red or green pepper, seeded, cored, and diced
3	tablespoons sour gherkins, diced
1	whole chicken breast, boiled and diced

After the rice is cooked, rinse in cold water. Drain thoroughly; set aside.

In large salad bowl, mix mustard, salt, and vinegar. Use a fork to blend and stir in the oil. Toss drained rice with dressing; coat well. Stir in remaining ingredients; mix gently. Serve salad cool, but not chilled. Makes 4 to 6 servings.

Cold Potato and Beet Salad

2	**fresh beets**
2	**medium potatoes**
½	**cup green onion, chopped**
¼	**cup olive oil**
3	**tablespoons wine vinegar**

1	**teaspoon dried sweet basil, crumbled**
½	**teaspoon dry mustard**
	Salt and pepper
1	**head Boston lettuce, cleaned**

Do not remove stalks from beets; just wrap them well in aluminum foil. Wash potatoes and prick with fork. Preheat oven to 450°F. Bake beets for 1 hour. Place potatoes in the oven and continue baking 1 hour more. Remove beets and potatoes from oven and allow to cool.

Remove skins from beets and potatoes and cut into 1/2-inch-thick slices. Combine beets, potatoes, and onions and mix gently. Combine the olive oil, wine vinegar, sweet basil, mustard, salt, and pepper and mix well. Pour over the beets and potatoes and mix gently. Refrigerate for several hours, covered, to mellow the flavors.

Serve at room temperature in a bowl garnished with the Boston lettuce. Makes 4 servings.

Marinated Vegetable Salad

2	**quarts water**
2	**teaspoons salt**
1	**(10-ounce) package Romano beans, partially defrosted**
1	**(10-ounce) package cauliflower**
2	**carrots, peeled and thinly sliced**
1	**medium zucchini, sliced ¼ inch thick**

2	**cloves garlic**
1	**teaspoon salt**
¼	**cup white wine vinegar**
6	**tablespoons olive oil**
¼	**teaspoon pepper**
½	**cup ripe olives, sliced**
1	**medium onion, peeled, sliced, and separated into rings**

Combine water and salt in Dutch oven; bring to boil. Add beans, cauliflower, and carrots; cook 4 minutes. Add zucchini and cook 3 minutes. Drain in colander.

Peel garlic cloves; place on wooden board. Sprinkle with salt and mash well with side of knife. Combine garlic, vinegar, oil, and pepper in bottom of salad bowl; mix well. Add vegetables, olives, and onion; mix gently. Cover and refrigerate several hours or overnight before serving. Makes 6 servings.

Pasta

Manicotti

Pasta
12 packaged manicotti shells
    or
12 cooked homemade
    manicotti noodles, 6
    inches square (see Index
    for Egg Noodles)
Boiling water

Filling
1 pound ricotta cheese or
    pot cheese
1 cup mozzarella, grated (¼
    pound)
¼ cup Parmesan cheese,
    grated
1 tablespoon dehydrated
    parsley flakes
1 egg, lightly beaten
½ teaspoon salt
¼ teaspoon white pepper
½ teaspoon garlic powder

Sauce
3 cups marinara sauce
½ cup water (omit water if
    using homemade noodles)
3 tablespoons Parmesan
    cheese, grated

If using the manicotti shells, cover with boiling water and let stand 5 minutes (you may cook homemade manicotti noodles in boiling, salted water before stuffing, but it really isn't necessary and they break very easily when cooked and stuffed). Drain and rinse in cold water. Set aside while making the filling.

Combine all of the filling ingredients and mix well.

Combine the marinara sauce and water (omit water if using homemade noodles) in a medium saucepan and heat on low while stuffing the noodles. Stuff each shell or pancake with 1/3 to 1/2 cup of filling. Pour 3/4 cup of the heated sauce into a 13 × 9 × 2-inch baking dish and tilt to coat lightly. Place stuffed noodles in the dish. Top with remaining sauce. Makes 4 servings.

Venetian-Style Manicotti

1 **(8-ounce) package manicotti noodles**	1 **teaspoon sweet basil, crumbled**
Boiling salted water	**Salt and pepper**
1 **tablespoon cooking oil**	

Meat Filling

Manicotti Sauce

1 **pound meatloaf mixture (ground pork, beef, and veal)**
6 **tablespoons butter**
6 **tablespoons flour**
1 **large onion, peeled and diced**
½ **teaspoon salt**
White pepper
1 **clove garlic, peeled and minced**
¼ **teaspoon ground nutmeg**
1½ **cups chicken broth**
1 **egg, well beaten**
1 **cup light cream**
1 **cup fresh bread crumbs**
¾ **cup Parmesan cheese, freshly grated**
¼ **cup parsley, finely chopped**
Nutmeg
Parsley, chopped

Cook manicotti shells in large pan of boiling salted water, with oil floating on surface, 15 minutes, until al dente. Drain well, rinse with cold water. Set aside.

In heavy skillet, cook meatloaf mixture, onion, and garlic over low heat until meat loses all red color. Break meat into small chunks as it cooks. Drain well. Combine meat mixture, egg, bread crumbs, parsley, and seasonings; mix well. Stuff manicotti shells with filling. Place in lightly greased baking dish.

Melt butter in large saucepan. Add flour; cook, stirring constantly, until bubbly. Add seasonings and stir well. Add broth and cream all at once. Cook, stirring constantly, until thickened. Remove from heat; stir in cheese. Pour sauce evenly over stuffed manicotti noodles. Sprinkle lightly with nutmeg and chopped parsley. Bake at 350°F 30 minutes. Serve immediately. Makes 6 to 8 servings.

Egg Noodles

1⅓ **cups flour**	2 **teaspoons olive oil**
½ **teaspoon salt**	2 **teaspoons water**
2 **eggs**	

Combine flour and salt in mixing bowl. Make a well in center.

Beat eggs, oil, and water together; pour into well. Mix thoroughly; add a little more water if necessary to form a stiff dough. Turn out onto lightly floured surface. Knead to form smooth, elastic dough (about 15 minutes). Let rest, covered, 30 minutes.

To roll by hand: Divide dough into 4 equal parts. Lightly flour a

Egg Noodles

smooth surface. Roll dough 1/4 at a time until it is as thin as you can roll it. Ideally it should be 1/16th inch thick. Select a ball-bearing rolling pin if possible, since it is very easy to get blisters. Cut according to recipe of your choice.

To roll by pasta machine: Let dough rest without kneading; divide into quarters. Take dough, 1/4 at a time, and pass through machine with rollers set as far apart as possible (usually number 10 or highest numerical setting on machine). Fold dough into thirds; pass through again. After passing dough through machine 10 times, turn setting down one notch; roll through. Continue to roll dough, reducing setting one notch each time, until desired thickness is achieved. The dough strip will become long. Do not fold it. If it becomes unwieldly, cut it in half and roll pieces separately. Roll to slightly less than 1/16th inch thick. Cut as directed above; dry.

Noodles can be prepared ahead. Simply roll them, cut, and dry for 1/2 hour, then freeze. It is best to quick-freeze noodles on a tray, then carefully transfer them to a bag or box; seal. Remove from freezer when ready to use. Cook same as freshly made pasta.

To cook, bring 4 to 5 quarts salted water to boil. Float 1 tablespoon oil on surface of water. Add pasta a few pieces at a time; stir. Cook until pasta floats to surface of water. Test for doneness. It should be firm, not mushy. Drain well. Yield for these pasta recipes is based on machine-rolled pasta. If you are rolling the dough by hand, make twice the amount of dough, since the product will not be as thin. Makes about 3/4 pound.

Green Noodles: Omit water. Add 1/4-cup well-drained, cooked, pureed spinach. Proceed as above.

Agnolotti with Cream Sauce

Pasta Dough
2 cups all-purpose flour
1 teaspoon salt
3 eggs
2 teaspoons olive oil
1 tablespoon water

Pasta Filling
2 tablespoons olive oil
¼ cup onion, finely chopped
¼ pound ground veal
1 egg
1 cup cooked chicken breast, finely chopped
⅛ pound prosciutto, finely chopped
¼ teaspoon rosemary, crushed
⅛ teaspoon nutmeg
Salt and pepper

Cream Sauce
3 tablespoons butter
6 tablespoons flour
Salt
Pepper
1½ cups chicken broth
1½ cups light cream
½ cup Parmesan cheese, freshly grated
⅛ teaspoon ground nutmeg

Prepare pasta dough. Combine flour and salt in mixing bowl. Combine eggs, oil, and water; mix well. Add to flour; mix to form stiff dough. Turn out onto board and knead 5 minutes. Cover with plastic wrap; let rest 30 minutes.

Prepare filling while dough rests. Heat oil in small, heavy skillet. Add onion; sauté until tender. Add veal. Cook, stirring, until meat is crumbly and lightly browned. Transfer mixture to mixing bowl; cool slightly. Add remaining filling ingredients and mix well.

Divide pasta dough into 4 parts. Cover any dough not being used, to prevent drying. Roll dough, 1 part at a time, on lightly floured surface to 1/16 inch thick. Cut into 3-inch circles with round cutter or glass. Reroll scraps. Place heaping 1/2 teaspoon filling on each round. Dampen edge of circle with a little water. Fold into half-moon shape; seal. With folded edge toward you, bring 2 ends together; pinch. (Finished pasta looks like small circular hats with cuffs.) Place pasta on tray; cover with towel until ready to cook, or freeze for future use.

Prepare sauce. Melt butter in medium saucepan. Add flour, salt, and pepper; mix well. Cook 1 minute. Gradually stir in broth. Cook, stirring constantly, until thickened; remove from heat. Stir in cream. Return to heat; cook, stirring constantly, until thickened. Add cheese and nutmeg. Keep sauce warm while cooking pasta.

Cook pasta 10 minutes in large amount boiling salted water, with small amount of oil added. Drain well. Serve immediately, topped with cream sauce. Sprinkle with additional Parmesan, if desired. Agnolotti can also be served with marinara sauce. Makes 6 servings.

Note: If available, use pasta machine for rolling dough.

Lasagne

Lasagne

9   lasagne noodles
2   onions, peeled and
    chopped
¾   pound ground meat
1   (14-ounce) can crushed
    tomatoes
1   tablespoon tomato paste
1   bouillon cube
½   teaspoon salt
¼   teaspoon white or black
    pepper
About 1 teaspoon crushed
    oregano or basil

Cheese Sauce
3   tablespoons butter or
    margarine
5   tablespoons flour
3⅓ cups milk
½ to 1 teaspoon salt
Black pepper
Ground nutmeg
1¼ cups cheese, grated

Boil the lasagne noodles.

Make meat sauce: Brown the onions and meat in a frying pan, while stirring so that it becomes a crumbled mixture. Add tomatoes, tomato paste, bouillon cube, and salt and pepper. Cover and simmer 20 to 30 minutes. Season with oregano or basil toward end of the simmering time.

Make cheese sauce: Melt butter and stir in flour. Add milk and bring to a boil while stirring constantly. Let sauce boil for 3 to 5 minutes. Stir in cheese and season with salt, pepper, and ground nutmeg.

Alternate lasagna noodles with meat sauce and cheese sauce in a greased, ovenproof dish. Start and finish with cheese sauce. Three layers of pasta is usually about right. Finally, sprinkle plenty of grated cheese on top.

Bake for 15 to 20 minutes at 425°F if the dish has just been prepared and the sauces are still warm. Bake it for 30 to 40 minutes at 400°F if the lasagne is cold. Makes 4 servings.

Venetian-Style Cannelloni

Pasta
½ recipe Egg Noodles (see Index)
4 quarts boiling salted water
1 tablespoon oil

Filling
1 large onion, chopped
1 clove garlic, minced
2 tablespoons olive oil
1 (10-ounce) package frozen chopped spinach, thawed
2½ cups ground cooked ham
2 eggs, beaten
¾ teaspoon dried oregano, crumbled
½ teaspoon salt
¼ teaspoon pepper

Sauce
⅓ cup butter or margarine
⅓ cup all-purpose flour
½ teaspoon salt
Dash nutmeg
Dash white pepper
1 cup chicken broth
1 cup light cream
½ cup Parmesan or Romano cheese, grated
1 cup white Cheddar or Swiss cheese, grated

Prepare the pasta according to the recipe. Allow to rest, covered, and roll on a lightly floured surface into sheets 1/16th of an inch thick; cut into 4 × 4-inch pieces. Allow to dry on lightly floured cookie sheets for 30 minutes. Float the oil on the surface of the water. Cook the pasta in the boiling water for 5 to 7 minutes or until al dente. Drain well and pat dry with paper towels.

Next make the filling. Sauté onions and garlic in oil until tender. Press the thawed spinach firmly in a strainer to remove all water. Combine onion mixture, spinach, ham, eggs, and seasonings in a large bowl and mix well. Fill the noodles with 3 tablespoons of the filling and roll jelly-roll fashion to form a cylinder. Place in a single layer in a shallow baking dish.

Next make the sauce: In a medium-size saucepan, melt the butter. Blend in flour and seasonings. Cook, stirring constantly, until bubbly. Add chicken broth and cream, all at one time, stirring well. Cook over moderate heat, stirring constantly, until thickened and smooth. Remove from heat and add cheese. Stir until cheese has melted. Pour the sauce evenly over the cannelloni. Bake in a 350°F oven for 30 minutes. Garnish with finely chopped parsley and paprika. Makes 15 stuffed noodles (serves 4 to 5).

Linguine with White Clam Sauce

18 fresh cherrystone clams	¼ teaspoon dried sweet basil, crumbled
1 tablespoon butter	
1 tablespoon olive oil	¼ teaspoon garlic powder
1 tablespoon flour	Salt and pepper to taste
¾ cup water or clam juice	1 tablespoon parsley, chopped
¼ teaspoon dried oregano, crumbled	
	12 ounces linguine

Scrub clams well under running water. Place on baking sheet and bake at 450°F until clams open. Remove clams from shells and chop. Reserve juice for the sauce or for another use.

Heat butter and oil in a medium saucepan. Stir in flour and cook, stirring constantly, for 2 minutes. Gradually stir water or clam juice into flour mixture. Mix well and continue to cook until thickened.

Add clams and seasonings and simmer 2 minutes. Add parsley and serve over hot cooked linguine. Makes 3 to 4 servings.

Ravioli

Pasta

1 double recipe Egg Noodles (see Index)

Ravioli Filling

¾ pound meatloaf mix	1 egg
¼ cup dry bread crumbs	1 tablespoon dehydrated parsley flakes
2 tablespoons Parmesan cheese, grated	½ teaspoon garlic salt
	¼ teaspoon pepper
	Cornmeal
	4 quarts boiling water
	1 tablespoon salt
	1 tablespoon cooking oil

Prepare the pasta according to the recipe; let rest, covered, 15 minutes. Combine filling ingredients in a bowl; mix well. Refrigerate until ready to use. Divide dough into 8 pieces. Roll 1 piece at a time on lightly floured surface. Keep remainder of dough tightly covered. Roll dough as thin as possible. If using a pasta machine to roll dough, roll it to slightly less than 1/16th inch thick. Cut dough into 2-inch squares. Place 1 teaspoon of filling in center of half of the squares. Top with remainder of squares. Press edges together tightly to seal. Moisten edges with a little water if necessary to ensure a tight seal. Dust cookie sheet lightly with cornmeal. Place ravioli on sheet. Refrigerate, covered, or freeze until ready to cook.

To cook, heat 4 quarts of water to boiling. Add salt, and float oil on surface of water. Drop ravioli into water a few at a time; stir to prevent them from sticking to bottom of pan. Reduce heat so that water boils gently. Cook approximately 12 minutes, until tender; drain.

Serve hot with your favorite tomato or meat sauce and grated cheese, or toss with melted butter and freshly grated Parmesan cheese. Makes 6 to 8 servings.

Gnocchi

2 cups milk	½ cup Parmesan cheese, grated
1 tablespoon butter	
½ teaspoon salt	
Pinch of freshly grated nutmeg	*For Garnish*
Ground white pepper, to taste	2 tablespoons butter, melted
½ cup farina (or semolina)	1 tablespoon Parmesan cheese, grated
2 eggs, beaten	

Butter a cookie sheet and set aside. In a heavy saucepan, combine the milk, butter, salt, nutmeg, and pepper and bring to a boil over moderate heat. Slowly add the farina, stirring constantly. Reduce heat to low and cook until very thick and a spoon will stand unsupported in the center of the pan. Remove from heat. Add eggs and Parmesan cheese and mix well. Spread on the cookie sheet in a rectangle 1/2 inch thick. Refrigerate until firm.

Cut into rounds about 1-1/2 inches in diameter. Arrange in greased casserole or baking dish, slightly overlapping. Drizzle with melted butter and sprinkle with Parmesan cheese. Bake in preheated 350°F oven for 20 minutes. Serve hot. Makes 3 to 4 servings.

Ravioli

Macaroni with Sauce Amatrice

Sauce Amatrice
2 tablespoons olive oil
2 cloves garlic, peeled and minced
¼ pound salt pork, diced
1 small onion, chopped
¼ cup dry white wine
1 (28-ounce) can Italian plum tomatoes, drained and minced
1 teaspoon sugar
1 teaspoon chili powder
½ teaspoon paprika
½ teaspoon dried sweet basil, crumbled
½ teaspoon dried oregano, crumbled
Salt and pepper

Pasta
3 quarts water
1 tablespoon salt
1 tablespoon cooking oil
12 ounces penne or other macaroni
Parmesan cheese, grated

Heat oil in large saucepan. Add garlic, salt pork, and onion. Sauté until onion is tender. Add wine; cook until it has evaporated. Add tomatoes and spices. Simmer 20 minutes, uncovered.

Meanwhile, heat water to boiling. Add salt. Float oil on surface of water. Add penne; cook until al dente. Drain. Place in serving bowl; top with sauce. Serve with Parmesan cheese. Makes 4 servings.

Spaghetti with Meatballs

Meatballs
1 pound lean ground beef
½ cup Italian-style bread crumbs
1 egg, slightly beaten
1 tablespoon dried onion flakes
Salt and pepper
3 tablespoons cooking oil

Tomato Sauce
2 tablespoons olive oil
1 medium onion, chopped
1 clove garlic, minced
1 (28-ounce) can Italian-style peeled tomatoes
1 (6-ounce) can tomato paste
¾ cup water (or refill tomato-paste can)
1½ teaspoons mixed Italian herbs
1 teaspoon sugar
½ cup dry red wine
½ pound Italian sausage, cut in 1-inch pieces and browned, or
1 (4-ounce) can sliced mushrooms, drained

Spaghetti
12 ounces thin spaghetti
4½ quarts boiling salted water
1 tablespoon cooking oil

First make the meatballs. Combine ground beef, bread crumbs, egg, onion flakes, salt, and pepper. Mix well and form into meatballs the size of a walnut. Brown in cooking oil in a medium-sized skillet. Drain.

Next make the tomato sauce. Heat olive oil in large saucepan. Add

Spaghetti with Meatballs

onion and garlic and sauté 5 minutes. Puree the tomatoes in a blender or force through sieve. Add to the onion mixture with the tomato paste, water, seasonings, and wine. Bring to a boil and reduce heat to low. Add the meatballs and sausage or mushrooms. Simmer covered for 1 to 1-1/2 hours, or until thick.

Bring the salted water to a boil. Float the cooking oil on the surface of the water. Add spaghetti and stir with fork to prevent sticking. Cook according to package directions and drain. To serve in the Italian manner, separate the meats from the sauce. Toss the sauce and the spaghetti together to coat lightly. Serve the meats on a platter so that guests can serve themselves. Pass the grated Parmesan cheese. Makes 4 servings.

Main Courses

Stuffed Chicken

1   (6-pound) capon or
    roasting chicken
½   pound hot or sweet Italian
    sausage (either bulk or
    links with casings
    removed)
2   tablespoons olive oil
½   cup onion, finely chopped
1   clove garlic, peeled and
    chopped
1   cup raw long-grain rice
2   cups boiling water

1   cup cleaned, sliced fresh
    mushrooms (or substitute
    4-ounce can drained
    mushrooms)
1   teaspoon chicken-broth
    granules
¼   teaspoon dried sweet basil,
    crumbled
Salt and pepper
Olive oil for rubbing
6   medium potatoes, peeled

Wash chicken; pat dry.

In small skillet, sauté sausage in oil until lightly browned. Add onion and garlic; sauté until lightly browned. Add rice; cook, stirring, until opaque. Add water, mushrooms, broth granules, and seasonings; cover tightly. Reduce heat to low. Cook 15 to 20 minutes, until tender. Cool.

Stuff chicken with mixture. Truss body cavity shut. Stuff neck cavity; skewer shut. Pin wings close to body; tie legs together. Rub liberally with oil, salt, and pepper. Grease roasting pan; place chicken in pan. Roast at 350°F (25 minutes to the pound). One hour before chicken is done, add potatoes to roasting pan. Baste occasionally with pan juices. Makes 6 servings.

Chicken Marinara

1	(2½- to 3-pound) broiler-fryer chicken, cut up
½	cup flour
1	teaspoon salt
¼	teaspoon pepper
3	tablespoons butter or margarine
1	(15½-ounce) can marinara sauce or 2 cups homemade marinara sauce
1	teaspoon dried dillweed
2	tablespoons Parmesan cheese, grated

Combine flour, salt, and pepper in a brown paper bag. Add chicken a few pieces at a time and shake until coated with the flour mixture. Place chicken in a single layer in a shallow baking dish. Dot with butter. Bake at 450°F for 25 minutes.

Remove from the oven. Pour sauce over the chicken. Sprinkle with dillweed and cheese. Reduce heat to 350°F and bake 25 minutes more. Serve hot or cold. Makes 4 servings.

Chicken Parmesan with Mushroom Marsala Sauce

2 to 3	tablespoons olive oil
6 to 8	pats butter
1	cup seasoned bread crumbs
1	cup Parmesan cheese, freshly grated
1	tablespoon Herbes d'Provence (or herbs of your choice)
6	single chicken breasts (deboned)
1	cup flour seasoned with salt and pepper, on plate
2	eggs, beaten in medium-sized bowl

Mushroom Marsala Sauce

1	pound fresh mushrooms
3 to 4	tablespoons butter
⅓	cup Marsala wine (or to taste)

Pour oil in center of 12-inch frying pan. Place pats of butter around oil; heat slowly to cooking temperature. Combine bread crumbs, cheese, and herbs on plate. Wash and pat dry chicken. Coat with seasoned flour; dip in eggs. Coat with bread-crumb mixture. Set aside on waxed paper or rack; repeat procedure for all pieces. Let stand in refrigerator 2 to 3 hours.

Place all pieces in frying pan at same time; fry to golden brown. Pour sauce over chicken just before serving. To make sauce: Clean mushrooms; sauté in butter. Add wine and stir until hot (do not bring to boil). Makes 6 servings.

Breast of Chicken with Prosciutto

4 **individual chicken breasts (about ½ pound each), skinned, boned**	1 **small onion, minced**
	1 **clove garlic, minced**
Salt and pepper	½ **pound mushrooms, cleaned and sliced**
1 **teaspoon dried leaf sage, crumbled**	¼ **cup chicken broth**
¼ **pound prosciutto, thinly sliced**	¼ **cup white wine**
4 **tablespoons butter**	2 **tablespoons fresh parsley, chopped**

Place chicken between sheets of waxed paper; pound with flat side of cleaver or bottom of heavy bottle to form cutlets of even thickness. Remove waxed paper. Season with salt and pepper and sprinkle with sage. Evenly distribute ham on top of chicken. Fold in half; secure with toothpick.

Melt butter in heavy skillet. Add chicken; cook over moderate heat, turning until lightly browned. Remove from pan. Add onion and garlic to pan; cook 1 minute. Add mushrooms; cook until mushroom liquid evaporates. Return chicken to skillet; spoon mushrooms over them. Add chicken broth and wine; cover. Simmer 20 minutes. Transfer to platter; cover chicken with mushrooms. Pour over pan juices; sprinkle with parsley. Makes 4 servings.

Fried Chicken Italian

2½ **pounds chicken parts (drumsticks, thighs, breasts, and wings)**	2 **tablespoons milk**
	⅔ **cup dry bread crumbs**
⅓ **cup flour**	⅓ **cup Parmesan cheese, grated**
½ **teaspoon seasoned salt**	**Oil for frying**
¼ **teaspoon pepper**	**Parsley**
2 **eggs**	**Lemon slices**

Wash chicken and pat dry. Combine flour and seasoned salt and pepper in a paper bag and shake chicken a few pieces at a time in flour mixture until lightly coated. Beat eggs and milk together in a shallow bowl. On a piece of waxed paper, combine bread crumbs and Parmesan cheese. Dip floured chicken pieces in the egg and then the bread-crumb mixture, coating well.

Heat 1-1/2 inches of oil in a heavy skillet over moderate heat. Fry the chicken a few pieces at a time until golden brown. Drain on paper towels. Place on a baking sheet and bake at 350°F for 15 to 20 minutes, or until the juices run clear when pierced with a knife.

Garnish with parsley and lemon slices and serve with basil-flavored tomato sauce if you wish. Makes 4 servings.

Breast of Chicken with Prosciutto

Chicken Cacciatore

1 (3-pound) chicken	6 anchovy fillets, chopped
3 tablespoons vegetable oil	⅓ cup wine vinegar
1 clove garlic	1⅓ cups dry red wine
½ teaspoon salt	3 tablespoons tomato paste
¼ teaspoon pepper	½ cup chicken bouillon
1 teaspoon rosemary	

Cut chicken into serving pieces. Heat oil in large frying pan; sauté chicken and garlic 5 minutes. Turn chicken often. Remove garlic. Add salt, pepper, rosemary, anchovies, vinegar, and wine. Simmer, uncovered, until liquid is reduced by one-third.

Dissolve tomato paste in bouillon; pour over chicken. Simmer, covered, 20 minutes or until chicken is done. Makes 4 servings.

Linguine with Chicken Livers

2 onions, chopped	⅛ teaspoon crushed red pepper
2 slices bacon, diced	½ pound chicken livers, cut into quarters
2 tablespoons olive oil	1 tablespoon butter
1 teaspoon salt	1 pound linguine
Freshly ground black pepper	
2 cups Italian plum tomatoes (1-pound can)	

In saucepan, cook onions and bacon in oil until onions are soft. Add salt, pepper, and tomatoes. Use a wooden spoon to break up tomatoes. Let simmer 20 minutes. Stir in red pepper. Simmer until sauce thickens somewhat. Taste; adjust seasonings as desired.

In a medium-size skillet, sauté chicken livers in melted butter about 5 minutes. Stir so livers are thoroughly cooked. Place livers and butter in the sauce. Simmer at least 5 minutes.

Cook linguine al dente; drain. Spoon linguine into soup bowls. Cover with sauce and livers. Makes 4 to 6 servings.

Chicken Tetrazzini

1 stewing chicken, about 3 to 4 pounds	Salt and pepper
2 onions	6 to 8 mushrooms, sliced
2 carrots	3 to 4 tablespoons whipping cream
Parsley, thyme, and 1 bay leaf	¼ cup Parmesan cheese, grated
½ pound spaghetti	2 tablespoons dried bread crumbs
6 tablespoons butter	
Dash of garlic powder	2 tablespoons sliced almonds, browned
4 tablespoons flour	
½ cup white wine	

Chicken Tetrazzini

Cook chicken slowly in water with onions, carrots, and herbs until tender. Let cool in stock, if possible overnight. Remove skin and bones; cook them in stock until well flavored and reduced to 2 to 3 cups.

Boil spaghetti in usual way; finish in 1 tablespoon butter flavored with a little garlic powder. Place in ovenproof dish; keep warm.

Make sauce: Melt 4 tablespoons butter. Add flour. When blended, add 1-1/2 cups chicken stock. Bring to boil; cook 2 minutes. Add wine; simmer few minutes.

Meanwhile, cut cold chicken into long strips. Place in mound on spaghetti; sprinkle with salt and pepper. Cook mushrooms in 1 tablespoon butter 2 or 3 minutes; put on chicken. Add cream to sauce; check seasoning. Spoon sauce over dish; sprinkle top with cheese and crumbs. Bake in 400°F oven 10 to 15 minutes, until well heated and top is brown and crisp. Sprinkle almonds over top. Serve at once. Makes 4 to 6 servings.

Chicken with Sausage

1	(2-pound) frying chicken, cut up	1	(16-ounce) can Italian-style plum tomatoes, broken up with fork
3	tablespoons olive oil		
4	sweet Italian sausage links (½ pound)	3	tablespoons tomato paste
		½	cup red wine
1	medium onion, peeled and sliced	1	teaspoon sweet basil, crumbled
1	large green pepper, cleaned and sliced		Pinch of sugar
			Salt and pepper
1	cup fresh mushrooms, sliced		

Wash chicken parts; pat dry. Heat oil in heavy skillet. Fry chicken, few pieces at a time, until golden, turning frequently. Remove from skillet; drain well. Add sausages to skillet; prick with fork. Fry until well browned. Remove from pan. Discard all but 3 tablespoons drippings.

Add onion, pepper, and mushrooms to skillet; sauté until tender. Add tomatoes, tomato paste, wine, and seasonings; stir well. Bring to boil. Add chicken and sausage. Cover; reduce heat to low. Cook 35 to 40 minutes. Serve with plain pasta. Makes 4 servings.

Turkey-Breast Cutlets with Lemon and Wine Sauce

2	tablespoons flour	Flour
3	tablespoons Parmesan cheese, freshly grated	4 tablespoons sweet butter
½	teaspoon salt	⅓ cup dry white wine
¼	teaspoon white pepper	Juice of ½ lemon
¼	teaspoon nutmeg	Chopped fresh parsley for garnish
1	egg, well beaten	Lemon wedges
½	cup milk	
1	pound raw boneless turkey breast	

In shallow bowl, combine flour, cheese, salt, pepper, and nutmeg. Add egg and milk; beat until well blended. Skin turkey breast; cut crosswise into 6 slices. Pound with meat mallet or side of plate until thin. Dredge lightly in flour; shake off excess. Heat butter in large heavy skillet over moderate heat until foam subsides. Dip turkey in batter and fry until golden. Remove from pan; keep warm.

When all turkey is cooked, add wine to skillet. Cook over low heat 2 minutes, stirring to loosen browned bits from pan. Add lemon juice; mix well. Pour sauce over turkey cutlets; sprinkle with chopped parsley. Serve immediately with lemon wedges. Makes 4 servings.

Turkey-Breast Cutlets with Lemon and Wine Sauce

Mixed Fish Fry

Mixed Fish Fry

Batter
3 large eggs
¼ cup olive oil
¼ cup all-purpose flour
¼ teaspoon dried rosemary, crumbled
¼ teaspoon dried sweet basil, crumbled
Salt and pepper

Fish Fry
1½ pounds fish fillets, shrimp, cleaned squid, clams, mussels, or eel (if fish is frozen, defrost and drain well)
Oil for frying (half olive oil, if possible)
½ cup flour
Salt and pepper
Parsley, lemon wedges, and quartered tomatoes

Beat eggs with whisk until well mixed. Add oil and beat to mix well. Add flour and seasonings; beat until smooth batter is formed. Let stand 30 minutes. Beat again before dipping fish.

Rinse fish; pat dry. Heat 3 inches oil in deep-fat fryer or 1 inch oil in electric skillet to 360°F. Dredge fish in flour seasoned with salt and pepper. Coat well; shake off excess. Dip fish in batter few pieces at a time. Deep-fat fry until golden. Drain on absorbent paper. Keep warm until all fish is cooked. Garnish with parsley and lemon wedges. Makes 6 servings.

Parmesan-Baked Halibut with Zucchini

1½ **pounds fillets of halibut**	***Garnish***
2 **cups fish broth**	⅓ **cup Parmesan cheese,**
1 **zucchini**	**freshly grated**
	⅓ **cup day-old white bread**
Sauce	**crumbs**
¾ **cup broth from the above**	1 **egg yolk plus ⅓ cup heavy**
¼ **cup dry white wine**	**cream**
⅓ **cup heavy cream**	

Boil fish broth in a low, wide pan and poach fish fillets in the broth for 2 to 4 minutes. Then place them on a large, ovenproof plate or on individual serving plates.

Thinly slice zucchini. Place the slices in salted boiling water. Let water come to a boil again, then drain the water and cool off the slices in cold water.

Prepare the sauce by mixing fish broth, wine, and cream in a pan. Bring sauce to a boil, then let simmer until it has a thick, creamy consistency. Pour sauce over the fish. Place zucchini slices on top. Mix cheese and white bread crumbs together and cover entire dish with them.

Preheat oven to 450°F. Beat egg yolk and cream together and sprinkle drops of this mixture over crumb mixture, using a fork to mix it in. Finally sprinkle a little more Parmesan cheese on top and bake in the oven until dish has browned. Makes 6 servings.

Ziti with Sardine Sauce

2 **tablespoons butter**	½ **teaspoon salt**
2 **tablespoons olive oil**	**Generous dash of freshly**
2 **small white onions, peeled**	**ground black pepper**
and minced	½ **cup clam juice**
2 **fresh basil leaves, minced**	6 **large black olives, sliced**
4 **ripe tomatoes, peeled and**	1 **tablespoon pignolia (pine**
diced	**nuts)**
1 **pound fresh sardines, cut**	1 **pound ziti tagliati**
into 2-inch pieces	

Heat butter and oil in medium-size saucepan. Add onions, basil, and tomatoes; simmer until onions are soft. Add sardine pieces. Use wooden spoon to break up tomatoes and sardines as they cook. Season with salt and pepper to taste. Add clam juice a little at a time by tablespoons; stir to blend all flavors. Simmer gently about 25 minutes. Sauce will be smooth and not watery. Add olives and pine nuts; simmer 10 minutes.

While sauce simmers, cook ziti al dente; drain. Place in warmed bowl. Add 1/2 of sauce; toss gently to blend. Spoon into individual portions. Spoon remaining sauce on top. Makes 6 servings.

Fish Stew

3 quarts water	2 pounds fish fillets (any firm white fish can be used; select one or more kinds from this list of possibilities: red snapper, bass, rockfish, cod, haddock, flounder, or perch), cut into chunks
1 tablespoon salt	
1 large onion, sliced	
1 bay leaf	
3 stalks celery (with tops), chopped	
1 (1¼-pound) lobster	
½ pound shrimp	2 cups drained Italian-style tomatoes, broken up
3 pounds fish heads, bones and trimmings	
1 dozen clams	1 cup dry white wine
½ cup olive oil	¼ cup parsley, chopped
2 cloves garlic, peeled and minced	¼ teaspoon thyme
	1 teaspoon dried sweet basil, crumbled
	Freshly ground pepper
	A scant ¼ teaspoon of saffron

In large stock pot (5 to 6 quarts), combine water, salt, onion, bay leaf, and celery and bring to a boil. Add lobster and return to a boil. Reduce heat to low and cook 10 minutes. Add shrimp and cook 5 minutes more. Remove shrimp and lobster. Add fish heads and trimmings and cook, uncovered, 1 hour. When shrimp and lobster are cool enough to handle, remove shrimp from shells and add the shells to the stock. Remove sand veins and discard.

Clean lobster and remove shell. Add shell to stock and cut meat into large chunks. Scrub clams and wash well to remove grit. Add to stock and cook 15 minutes. Remove from pot and reserve.

In a Dutch oven, heat olive oil. Add garlic and sauté until lightly browned. Add fish and brown in oil. Add tomatoes, wine, parsley, thyme, basil, and pepper and stir well.

Strain fish stock through a fine sieve. You should have 2 quarts. Dissolve saffron in the broth. Add to fish and tomato mixture. Bring to a boil. Reduce heat to low and cook 15 minutes. Add lobster, shrimp, and clams and cook 10 minutes more. Serve in large soup bowls. Makes 4 servings.

Salt Cod Venetian-Style

1½ pounds salt cod	1½ cups milk
¾ cup olive oil	Freshly ground pepper
2 medium onions, peeled and sliced	2 tablespoons parsley, chopped
1 clove garlic, peeled and minced	2 tablespoons Parmesan cheese, grated
Flour	

Fish Stew

Place cod in cold water to cover. Soak 24 hours; change water several times. Drain well. Skin and bone cod. Cut into serving-size pieces.

Heat oil in heavy skillet. Add onions and garlic; sauté until tender.

Lightly dredge cod in flour. Tightly pack into shallow casserole dish. Pour onion mixture over cod. Add milk to casserole. Sprinkle with pepper, parsley, and cheese. Cover tightly with foil. Bake at 250°F 4-1/2 hours, stirring occasionally. Makes 4 or 5 servings.

Spaghetti with Clams and Anchovies

2	white onions, peeled and chopped	10	ripe tomatoes, peeled and chopped
2	tablespoons olive oil	2	small green peppers, chopped
30	shucked cherrystone clams and liquid	1	clove garlic, peeled and minced
6	anchovy fillets, drained	1	pound spaghetti

Use medium to large saucepan to sauté onions in oil. When onions are soft and transparent, add clam liquid and anchovies. Simmer 8 minutes. Add tomatoes, green peppers, and garlic. Cook until about 1/2 of liquid has been absorbed, about 30 minutes. Add clams; cook 5 minutes.

Cook spaghetti al dente; drain. Place into warm bowl. Pour sauce over spaghetti; toss to mix. Serve in hot bowls so that every bit of sauce can be spooned up. Makes 4 to 6 servings.

Shrimp with Marinara Sauce

1	pound large shrimp (18 to 22)	**Sauce**	
1	quart water	2	tablespoons olive oil
Salt		½	cup onion, chopped
1	bay leaf	1	clove garlic, minced
1	slice lemon	1½	cups Italian-style plum tomatoes, peeled
¼	cup tomato puree		
½	teaspoon sugar	**Garnish**	
½	teaspoon dried sweet basil, crumbled	2	tablespoons dry bread crumbs
Salt and pepper		2	tablespoons Parmesan cheese, grated
		1	tablespoon parsley, finely chopped

Peel and devein shrimp. Combine water, salt to taste, bay leaf, and lemon in a large saucepan. Bring to a boil. Add shrimp; bring the water rapidly to a boil and cook 5 minutes. Drain.

Heat oil in a heavy skillet. Add onion and garlic and sauté until tender. Break up tomatoes, and add to the onion and garlic along with the tomato puree and seasonings. Reduce heat to low and cook uncovered 20 minutes.

Place shrimp in lightly greased au gratin dish. Top with sauce. Combine bread crumbs, cheese, and parsley and sprinkle over top of the shrimp and sauce. Preheat oven to 450°F and bake for 10 minutes. Makes 3 servings.

Spaghetti with Clams and Anchovies

Shrimp Scampi

2 **pounds large or jumbo shrimp, raw, in shells**	½ **teaspoon freshly ground pepper**
¾ **cup olive oil**	¼ **cup parsley, chopped**
2 **cloves garlic, crushed**	**Lemon wedges**
1 **teaspoon salt**	

Wash shrimp well. Slit down back almost to tail with very sharp knife. Devein shrimp; leave shell intact. Place in single layer in shallow pan. Combine oil, garlic, salt, and pepper; pour over shrimp. Cover; refrigerate 2 hours.

Thread 4 or 5 shrimp (depending on size) on each skewer. Grill over hot charcoal fire or in broiler (4 inches from heat source) 4 to 5 minutes on each side. Baste with oil in which shrimp were marinated. Serve immediately, sprinkled with parsley, topped with lemon wedges. Makes 6 servings.

Shrimp, Lobster, and Crab Diavolo

1 **(1¼-pound) live lobster**	2 **cloves garlic, peeled and minced**
1 **pound king crab legs**	
2 **pounds medium shrimp, raw**	⅛ **teaspoon crushed red pepper**
½ **cup butter**	**Juice of 1 lemon**
2 **tablespoons olive oil**	2 **tablespoons parsley, chopped**

Steam lobster and crab legs and cool. Peel shrimp, leaving tails intact. Butterfly, and remove sand vein. Drain well. Remove lobster and crab from the shell and slice.

In large heavy skillet, heat butter and oil over moderate heat. Add garlic and sauté for 2 minutes. Add shrimp and pepper and sauté until shrimp turns pink. Add crab and lobster and heat through. Sprinkle with lemon juice and parsley and serve with garlic bread. Makes 4 to 5 servings.

Fried Squid

3 **pounds frozen squid**	1 **teaspoon salt**
2 **cups Italian-style bread crumbs**	½ **teaspoon pepper**
	3 **eggs, well beaten**

Thaw squid. Remove tentacles by cutting them from head; reserve. Remove and discard head, chitinous pen, and viscera. Wash thoroughly; drain. Cut mantle into rings.

Combine bread crumbs, salt, and pepper. Dip tentacles and mantle rings in egg, then in crumbs; coat well. Deep-fat fry at 350°F until golden brown. Serve immediately with lemon wedges. Makes 4 or 5 servings.

Shrimp Scampi

Beef Parma-Style

1½ **pounds beef round steak**	1 **(6-ounce) can tomato paste**
½ **cup dry bread crumbs**	2 **cups hot water**
⅓ **cup Parmesan cheese, grated**	½ **teaspoon dried marjoram, crumbled**
1 **egg**	1 **teaspoon salt**
2 **tablespoons water**	¼ **teaspoon pepper**
¼ **cup flour**	½ **pound mozzarella cheese, thinly sliced**
⅓ **cup cooking oil**	
1 **medium onion, minced**	

Place meat between sheets of waxed paper; pound with heavy skillet on hard surface until quite thin. Cut into serving-size pieces. Combine bread crumbs and Parmesan cheese. Beat egg and 2 tablespoons water together. Dip meat in flour; turn to coat; shake off excess. Dip meat in egg mixture, then in crumb mixture. Pat crumbs into meat to coat well.

Heat oil in heavy skillet over moderate heat. Brown the meat on both sides. Remove from pan. Add onion to pan; brown lightly. Add tomato paste, hot water, and seasonings; stir well. Boil 5 minutes.

Place meat in shallow baking dish. Cover with sauce; reserve 3/4 cup. Top meat with mozzarella cheese. Pour remaining sauce over cheese. Cover with aluminum foil. Bake at 350°F 2 hours. Serve with pasta and a green salad. Makes 4 or 5 servings.

Beef Rolls with Tomato Gravy

1¼ **pounds top round of beef, very thinly sliced (¼ inch thick)**	1½ **cups canned Italian-style plum tomatoes, peeled and broken up**
¼ **cup olive oil**	½ **cup tomato sauce**
1 **medium onion, finely chopped**	½ **tablespoon dehydrated parsley flakes**
¾ **cup Italian-style bread crumbs**	½ **teaspoon sugar**
3 **tablespoons olive oil**	½ **teaspoon oregano**
2 **tablespoons onion, chopped**	**Salt and pepper**

Pound meat well; cut into rectangular pieces approximately 4 × 6 inches. You should have 8 pieces, so vary the measurements accordingly. Heat 1/4 cup olive oil in small skillet. Sauté onion until tender. Remove from heat. Add bread crumbs and stir well. Place 2 tablespoons bread-crumb mixture on each piece of meat; roll jelly-roll fashion to enclose stuffing. Fasten with toothpicks.

Beef Rolls with Tomato Gravy

Heat 3 tablespoons olive oil in heavy skillet. Brown steak rolls. Place in shallow baking dish. Add onion to skillet; brown lightly. Add remaining ingredients and stir well. Simmer 15 to 20 minutes or until thickened. Pour over the steak rolls; cover. Bake at 350°F 1 hour. Serve with mashed potatoes. Makes 4 servings.

Beef Stew

2 tablespoons olive oil	½ teaspoon dried sweet basil, crumbled
2 slices bacon, chopped	Salt and pepper
½ cup onion, chopped	½ teaspoon sugar
½ cup celery, sliced	3 medium carrots, peeled
1 clove garlic, minced	and sliced
1¼ pounds lean stew beef, cut into 1-inch cubes	3 medium potatoes, peeled and diced
2 tablespoons parsley, chopped	¼ cup red wine
1 (16-ounce) can peeled tomatoes, broken up	1½ cups zucchini squash (unpeeled), sliced
½ cup water	
1 teaspoon beef-broth granules	

Heat oil in Dutch oven. Add bacon and sauté until crisp. With slotted spoon remove bacon from pan; reserve. Add onion, celery, and garlic to pan; sauté 5 minutes. Remove with slotted spoon; reserve.

Add stew beef to pan. Cook over moderate heat until well browned on all sides; stir occasionally. Add reserved ingredients, parsley, tomatoes, water, beef-broth granules, and seasonings. Cook, covered, over low heat 1 hour. Add carrots and potatoes; stir well. Cover and cook 45 minutes. Add wine and zucchini; stir well. Cook 15 minutes or until vegetables are tender. Makes 4 servings.

Stuffed Peppers

4 medium bell peppers	1 (8-ounce) can tomato sauce
1 pound ground beef	¼ cup water
½ cup onion, chopped	1 cup instant rice (or quick-cooking)
½ teaspoon garlic powder	
1 teaspoon mixed Italian herbs, crumbled	2 ounces mozzarella cheese, thinly sliced
Salt and pepper	
1 (16-ounce) can stewed tomatoes	

Cut tops off peppers; remove seeds and membranes. Parboil peppers 5 minutes; drain.

Sauté beef and onion in large skillet until lightly browned; add a little oil if meat is very lean. Add garlic powder, Italian herbs, salt, pepper, tomatoes, 1/2 can of tomato sauce, water, and rice; stir well. Bring to boil. Reduce heat to low and cook, covered, 15 minutes.

Place peppers in 2-quart casserole. Stuff with meat mixture; spoon remaining mixture around peppers. Top with remaining tomato sauce. Cover and cook 30 minutes at 350°F. Uncover; top with cheese. Cook 10 minutes. Makes 4 servings.

Roast Leg of Lamb with Rosemary

1   **(5-pound) whole leg of lamb or sirloin half leg of lamb**
1   **large clove garlic**
1   **teaspoon dried rosemary, crumbled**
1   **teaspoon lemon peel, grated**
Salt and freshly ground black pepper
Olive oil

Wipe meat with damp cloth. Peel garlic; rub over surface of lamb Cut garlic clove into slivers. Make 4 or 5 deep slashes in meat; insert garlic slivers. Rub meat with rosemary, lemon peel, salt, and pepper. Place in open roasting pan on trivet, fat-side-up. Sprinkle with olive oil. Roast at 325°F 3 hours or to an internal temperature of 180°F. Let stand 10 minutes before carving.

Peeled potatoes and carrots can be placed in pan drippings for last 1-1/2 hours of cooking time; turn occasionally. Makes 6 servings.

Stuffed Peppers

Lamb Roast Roman-Style

1	(3-pound) boned, rolled lamb roast (leg or shoulder)
2	cloves garlic, peeled, cut into slivers
1	teaspoon dry rosemary, crumbled
½	teaspoon dry marjoram, crumbled
Freshly ground pepper	
3	slices bacon, cut in half

Anchovy Sauce

2	anchovy fillets
1½	tablespoons olive oil
1½	tablespoons lemon juice
1	tablespoon fresh bread crumbs
½	cup parsley, chopped
1	teaspoon lemon rind, freshly grated
½	teaspoon rosemary, crumbled

Wipe meat with damp cloth. Cut slits in top; place garlic sliver in each slit. Rub roast with rosemary, marjoram, and pepper. Place in roast pan, fat-side-up. Place bacon slices, slightly overlapping, over top of roast. Roast at 325°F 2-1/4 hours (internal temperature of 170°F). Roast should still be pink when sliced.

Prepare sauce while lamb cooks. Mash anchovy fillets with oil. Stir in lemon juice and bread crumbs. Add remaining ingredients; stir well. Refrigerate until ready for use. Serve lamb with sauce, steamed broccoli, and tomato salad. Potatoes can be pan-roasted with lamb. Makes 4 or 5 servings.

Venetian-Style Lamb Chops

2	tablespoons butter or margarine
2	tablespoons olive oil
4	lamb shoulder chops (approximately 2 pounds)
Salt and pepper to taste	
1	medium onion
1¾	pounds eggplant
3	tablespoons tomato paste

½	teaspoon dried sweet basil, crumbled
½	cup boiling water
½	(10-ounce) package frozen peas
1	(8½-ounce) can artichoke bottoms (or substitute 1 can artichoke hearts), drained

Heat butter and oil in heavy skillet. Wipe chops with damp cloth; season with salt and pepper. Sauté in butter and oil approximately 4 minutes per side, until well browned and almost done. Remove from pan; keep warm.

While chops cook, peel onion; quarter; separate layers. Cut stem from eggplant; cut in half lengthwise; thinly slice. Add the onion to the skillet; sauté 5 minutes. Add eggplant.

Combine tomato paste, basil, and boiling water; stir well. Add to skillet and bring to boil. Reduce heat to low; cover. Cook 15 minutes. Add peas, artichoke bottoms (quartered) or hearts, and lamb chops. Cook, covered, 15 minutes or until vegetables are done through. Makes 4 servings.

Venetian-Style Lamb Chops

Marinated Liver with Tomato-Crush

¾ cup red wine	½ teaspoon basil
1 teaspoon thyme	1½ teaspoons salt
4 to 6 slices calf liver	⅓ cup flour
4 tomatoes	¼ teaspoon black pepper
1 small onion	1 tablespoon butter or
1 tablespoon olive oil	margarine
2 cups celery, cut in strips	

Mix wine and thyme in a bowl. Place liver slices in the mixture and marinate for 1 hour in refrigerator.

Dip tomatoes in boiling water, then peel. Remove seeds and cut tomatoes into large pieces. Peel and mince onion. Heat oil in a little pot and lightly sauté onion. Add tomato pieces, celery, basil, and 1/2 teaspoon of salt. Simmer for a few minutes.

Dry off the liver. Dredge slices in flour that has been mixed with the remaining salt and pepper. Brown butter in a frying pan and sauté liver slices for about 3 minutes on each side.

Divide tomato mixture over the liver slices and serve immediately. Makes 4 servings.

Italian Sausages and Beans

1 **pound sweet or hot Italian sausage links**	2 **(16-ounce) cans cannelli beans or kidney beans, drained**
Cold water	
2 **tablespoons olive oil**	2 **tablespoons parsley, chopped**
¼ **cup onions, chopped**	
1 **(8-ounce) can tomato sauce**	

Prick sausages well on all sides. Place in large skillet and just barely cover with cold water. Cook over moderate heat, uncovered, until water evaporates. Then cook, turning occasionally, until sausages are browned on all sides. Remove from pan and keep warm.

Add oil and onion to skillet and sauté until tender. Add tomato sauce and simmer 5 minutes. Add beans and sausages to the pan and simmer for 15 minutes, stirring occasionally to prevent sticking. Sprinkle with parsley and serve. Makes 4 servings.

Sausage with Lentils

2 **cups dried lentils**	1 **bay leaf**
8 **cups water**	2 **teaspoons salt**
1 **ounce salt pork, diced**	**Freshly ground pepper**
2 **large tomatoes, peeled and diced**	1 **cotechino sausage or 1 zampone (about 2 pounds)**
1 **clove garlic, peeled**	

Wash lentils; pick over well to remove foreign matter. Place lentils in large saucepan. Add water, salt pork, tomatoes, garlic, bay leaf, salt, and pepper. Bring to boil over moderate heat. Skim foam from surface of cooking liquid; reduce heat to low. Simmer, uncovered; stir occasionally until lentils are soft and liquid almost evaporated. (Cooking time should be 45 minutes to 1 hour.) If liquid evaporates too quickly, add a little water.

Meanwhile, prick sausage well. Place in a large pot and add water to cover. Bring to boil. Reduce heat to low; simmer 1 hour, until tender. Remove from pan and cool slightly. Slice; place on platter.

Remove bay leaf and garlic clove from lentils. Spoon lentils around sausage and serve. Makes 6 servings.

Note: Cotechino and zampone are usually available in Italian delicatessens around the New Year. If unavailable, substitute 1½ pounds Italian sausage. Prick well; cook in ½ inch water until water evaporates; brown in own fat.

Sausage with Lentils

Piccata with Rice and Saffron Sauce

1 **pound fillet of pork or veal**	⅛ **teaspoon white pepper**
	¼ **cup flour**
	2 to 3 **tablespoons butter**

Batter
2 to 3 **eggs**
⅔ **cup Parmesan cheese, grated**
2½ **tablespoons water**
½ **teaspoon paprika**
½ **teaspoon salt**

Saffron Sauce
1⅓ **cups crème fraîche or sour cream**
Pinch saffron, crushed
½ to ¾ **teaspoon salt**
About 1 tablespoon butter

Trim fat and membranes from the meat; cut meat into 8 pieces. Flatten each using a pounder or a small thick-bottomed pot.

Mix eggs, cheese, water, and spices into a batter. Pour flour out on a plate and dredge slices of meat in the flour. In the meantime, heat a large frying pan to medium temperature.

Lightly brown butter in the pan. Dip meat slices in the egg batter, turning the slices so that both sides get covered, and place them in the frying pan. Sauté 1 to 2 minutes on each side, making sure that the pan does not get too hot. Cook slices in several batches if pan is not large enough.

Make saffron sauce. Bring crème fraîche to a boil. Season with saffron and salt. Boil the sauce for several minutes and then beat in 1 tablespoon cold butter.

Serve piccata on warm plates with a pool of saffron sauce and with rice as a side dish. Allow 2 meat slices per person. Makes 4 servings.

Pork Roast in Chianti

1 **(4-pound) pork roast, boned, rolled, and tied**	1 **teaspoon dried basil, crumbled**
1½ **cups Chianti wine**	3 **tablespoons olive oil**
1 **clove garlic, minced**	1 **(8-ounce) can tomato sauce**
2 **tablespoons lemon juice**	**Salt and pepper to taste**
1 **teaspoon dried rosemary, crumbled**	

Wipe pork roast with damp cloth. Place in glass or porcelain container or heavy-duty freezer bag. Combine Chianti, garlic, lemon juice, rosemary, and basil; pour over meat. Cover and marinate in refrigerator 24 hours. Turn occasionally (if using plastic bag, close with twist-tie). Bring roast to room temperature before cooking. Remove roast from marinade; pat dry. Reserve marinade.

Heat oil in large heavy Dutch oven. Brown roast well on all sides. Combine marinade and tomato sauce, salt, and pepper; pour over meat.

Piccata with Rice and Saffron Sauce

Bring to boil. Reduce heat to simmer and cover. Cook 3 hours (meat should be fork-tender). Place roast on platter and slice. Serve with pan juices. Makes 6 to 8 servings.

Breaded Pork Chops

Breaded Pork Chops

4 loin pork chops, 1 inch thick	2 tablespoons water
Salt and pepper	Bread crumbs
1 large egg	¼ cup clarified butter
	½ teaspoon dried sage

Carefully trim excess fat from pork chops. Season with salt and pepper.

Beat egg and water together. Dip chops in egg, then coat with bread crumbs. Press crumbs firmly onto chops.

In heavy skillet, heat butter over moderate heat. Crumble sage; add to butter. Add chops; cook slowly until well browned and done through. Makes 4 servings.

Stuffed Breast of Veal

Stuffing

3	tablespoons olive oil
1	medium onion, chopped
½	pound fresh spinach, stems removed and shredded
¼	pound ground veal
¼	pound ground pork
1	egg
½	cup fresh bread crumbs
¼	cup fresh pine nuts
⅛	teaspoon nutmeg
	Salt and pepper

Veal

1	(4- to 5-pound) veal breast, boned
	Salt and pepper
2	tablespoons olive oil
2	cups beef broth
½	cup white wine
1	carrot, peeled and sliced
1	stalk celery, chopped
2	bay leaves
	Salt and pepper
3	tablespoons cornstarch
3	tablespoons water

Heat oil in heavy skillet. Add onion; sauté until tender. Add spinach; sauté, stirring constantly, until wilted. Remove from heat; cool. Add remaining stuffing ingredients and mix well.

Have butcher cut pocket in veal breast for stuffing. Wipe meat with damp cloth. Season with salt and pepper on outside and in pocket. Fill pocket with stuffing; skewer shut. Heat oil in Dutch oven. Brown veal well on all sides. Add broth, wine, carrot, celery, and seasonings. Bring to boil; cover. Roast at 350°F. 2-1/2 hours; baste every 1/2 hour. Remove from oven. Take meat from pan; keep warm. Combine cornstarch and water; mix well. Add to pan juices; cook over low heat until thickened.

Remove skewer; carve veal breast. Serve with gravy. Makes 6 servings.

Veal with Marsala Wine

1	pound thinly sliced leg of veal or 1 pound tenderized unbreaded veal steaks
2	eggs
½	cup flour
	Salt and pepper

5	tablespoons butter (divided)
1	cup fresh mushrooms, thinly sliced
⅓	cup Marsala wine
⅔	cup beef broth

Lightly pound veal to an even thickness. Beat eggs well in shallow pie plate. Place meat in egg mixture. Let stand 30 minutes; turn occasionally. Combine flour, salt, and pepper to taste. Drain veal; dredge in flour mixture.

Heat 3 tablespoons butter in heavy skillet over medium heat until hot and foamy. Add veal; sauté, turning, until golden brown. Remove veal from pan; keep warm on platter. Melt remaining butter in skillet. Sauté mushrooms until tender. Add wine and beef broth; cook 5 minutes. Pour over veal. Makes 4 servings.

Veal Scallopini in Lemon Sauce

1¼ pounds veal for scallopini	¼ cup chicken broth
2½ tablespoons flour	¼ cup white wine
Salt	½ of a fresh lemon, thinly sliced
White pepper	
6 tablespoons clarified butter	1 tablespoon parsley, finely chopped

Arrange veal slices close together on a cutting board or waxed paper and lightly sprinkle with flour, salt, and white pepper. Turn and flour and season the other side of the meat. Heat clarified butter in large heavy skillet. Quickly brown veal a few pieces at a time on both sides.

Remove from pan and keep warm. Add chicken broth, wine, and lemon slices. Push lemon slices down into the liquid. Reduce heat to simmer, cover pan, and cook over low heat for 5 minutes. Place veal on a heated platter, pour sauce over the meat, and sprinkle with parsley. Makes 4 servings.

Veal Shanks Milanese

3 pounds veal shank, sawed into thick slices with marrow intact	½ cup white wine
	¼ cup chicken broth
	1 bay leaf
Salt and pepper	¼ teaspoon thyme
Flour	
6 tablespoons butter	*Gremolata*
1 medium onion, peeled and chopped	2 tablespoons parsley, finely chopped
1 clove garlic, peeled and minced	1 clove garlic, peeled and finely minced
2 carrots, peeled and diced	1 teaspoon lemon peel, finely grated
2 stalks celery, chopped	

Wipe veal with damp cloth. Season with salt and pepper. Dredge in flour; shake off excess. Heat butter in deep skillet or Dutch oven. Add veal; brown well on all sides. Remove from pan.

Add onion and garlic to pan; sauté until tender. Add vegetables, wine, chicken broth, and seasonings. Add veal shanks, standing on their sides to prevent marrow falling from bone during cooking. Bring mixture to a boil. Cover pan tightly; reduce heat to simmer. Cook approximately 1 hour, until veal is tender. If mixture looks dry at any time, add a little broth.

Meanwhile, combine gremolata ingredients; mix well. Transfer veal to heated platter. Pour sauce over meat; sprinkle with gremolata. Serve with risotto or plain cooked pasta. Makes 4 servings.

Milanese Veal Rolls

Milanese Veal Rolls

1½ pounds rump roast of veal
    or veal cutlet
Salt and pepper
Ground sage
4 slices prosciutto
8 thin slices mozzarella
    cheese
3 tablespoons olive oil
1 small onion, chopped

1 clove garlic, minced
1 (16-ounce) can Italian-
    style peeled tomatoes
½ cup white wine
Salt and pepper
8 thin strips mozzarella
    cheese
Parsley sprigs

Pound meat with a mallet to 1/8 inch thickness. Sprinkle with salt, pepper, and a little sage. Cut into 8 rectangular pieces. Cut slices of prosciutto in half. Top veal pieces with a piece of ham and a slice of mozzarella. Roll jelly-roll fashion and tie with string.

In a large skillet, heat oil and sauté veal rolls until browned. Remove from pan. Add onion and garlic and sauté until tender. Break tomatoes up with a fork and add to skillet, with the white wine and salt and pepper. Mix well. Add veal rolls and cover. Simmer 1-1/2 hours or until tender.

Top with the mozzarella strips; cover and melt the cheese.

Serve on a bed of hot cooked spaghetti, topped with the sauce and garnished with parsley sprigs. Makes 4 servings.

Mixed Boiled Meats with Green Sauce

Meat Pot
1 pound beef pot roast or brisket
1 pound veal shoulder
2 whole chicken legs
2 marrow bones, cracked
Water
2 bay leaves
1 onion
2 cloves
1 clove garlic
1 teaspoon salt
½ teaspoon sugar
4 peppercorns
½ teaspoon thyme
4 carrots, peeled and cut in half lengthwise
2 leeks, cleaned and cut in half lengthwise

½ pound cooked beef tongue
Parsley for garnish

Green Sauce
Juice of 1 fresh lemon
3 egg yolks
¼ teaspoon salt
½ cup olive oil
1 slice white bread, soaked in water and squeezed dry
½ teaspoon prepared mustard
1 clove garlic, peeled and mashed
½ cup parsley, chopped
½ teaspoon dried sweet basil, crumbled
½ teaspoon dried oregano, crumbled

Place beef, veal, chicken, and marrow bones in a large Dutch oven or stew pot. Cover with water. Add bay leaves. Peel onion and stud it with cloves, and add to the kettle. Peel clove of garlic, sprinkle with salt, and mash with blade of a knife. Add to the pot with the sugar, peppercorns, and thyme. Bring to a boil. Skim foam from surface of the liquid. Reduce heat to low, cover, and cook for 40 minutes. Remove chicken, add carrots and leeks, and cook for 30 more minutes.

Meanwhile, make the green sauce. Combine lemon juice, egg yolks, and salt in the jar of an electric blender. Blend on medium speed for 2 minutes. Add oil a tablespoon at a time, blending well after each addition. Add bread, mustard, and garlic and blend 2 minutes. Pour into a serving bowl and stir in the parsley, sweet basil, and oregano. Refrigerate until serving time.

Skin the chicken. Return to the pot along with the tongue and heat through. Remove the meats from the pot and slice. Arrange on a warm platter, garnish with parsley, and serve with the green sauce. Reserve the broth for soups. Makes 4 large servings.

Veal Shanks Milanese

Vegetables and Rice

Mixed Vegetables in the Italian Manner

2 tablespoons olive oil	1 medium zucchini, cut into ½-inch slices
1 medium onion, peeled and chopped	3 medium tomatoes, peeled and quartered
1 clove garlic, peeled and minced	¼ teaspoon dried rosemary, crumbled
1 green pepper, cleaned and cut into chunks	¼ teaspoon dried basil, crumbled
1 red pepper, cleaned and cut into chunks	Salt and pepper
½ pound eggplant (1 small or ½ of a large eggplant), unpeeled and cut into chunks	

Heat olive oil in large skillet. Add onion and garlic and saute until both are transparent. Add peppers, eggplant, zucchini, tomatoes, and seasonings and bring to a boil. Reduce heat to low and cook until vegetables are tender. Makes 3 to 4 servings.

Roman-Style Green Beans

1	(9-ounce) package frozen French-cut green beans	¼	teaspoon dried oregano, crumbled
1	tablespoon fresh lemon juice	⅛	teaspoon garlic powder
2	tablespoons olive oil		Salt and pepper
		¼	cup black olives, sliced

Cook beans in boiling salted water according to package directions. Drain well. Meanwhile, combine lemon juice, olive oil, seasonings, and olives in small saucepan and heat through. Pour over the cooked beans and toss well. Serve immediately. Makes 4 servings.

Mushrooms with Garlic and Oil

1	pound fresh mushrooms	2	cloves garlic
2	tablespoons olive oil	¼	teaspoon salt

Clean mushrooms with damp cloth, or, if necessary, wash in cold water. Remove stems and reserve for another use. Pat dry. Cut large mushrooms in quarters. Cut medium-size mushrooms in half and leave small ones whole.

Heat oil over moderate heat in heavy skillet. Peel garlic cloves and slice. Sauté garlic in oil until lightly browned. Remove garlic from pan with slotted spoon. Sprinkle oil with salt. Add mushrooms and sauté over moderately high heat until liquid coming from the mushrooms has evaporated. Stir constantly to prevent sticking.

Reduce heat to low and cook uncovered for 40 minutes, stirring occasionally, until mushrooms are golden. Serve with steak or other meat dishes. Makes 4 servings.

Sautéed Sweet Peppers

3	tablespoons olive oil	1	pound tomatoes, peeled and cut into chunks
1	clove garlic, peeled		Salt and pepper
2	large green peppers, cleaned and cut into strips		Chopped parsley
2	large red peppers, cleaned and cut into strips		

Heat oil in heavy skillet. Add garlic and cook over moderate heat until browned; discard. Add peppers; sauté, stirring constantly, 5 minutes. Add tomatoes and salt and pepper to taste. Simmer, uncovered, until mixture is thick.

Serve hot or cold garnished with parsley. Makes 4 servings.

Romano Beans in Tomato Sauce

2 tablespoons olive oil	½ cup tomato sauce
1 small clove garlic, minced	Salt and pepper
2 tablespoons onion, chopped	2 tablespoons water
¼ cup prosciutto or baked ham, minced	1 (9-ounce) package frozen Italian (or Romano) green beans

Heat oil in medium saucepan. Add garlic, onion, and prosciutto; sauté 5 minutes. Add tomato sauce, salt, pepper, and water; mix well. Add frozen beans; bring to boil. Stir to break up beans; cover. Reduce heat to low; cook 15 minutes. Makes 3 or 4 servings.

Fried Eggplant

1 medium eggplant (about 1 pound)	¾ cup dry bread crumbs
1 egg	2 tablespoons Parmesan cheese, grated
2 tablespoons water	Cooking oil
⅓ cup flour	

Peel eggplant and cut into 1/2-inch slices. Soak in cold salted water to cover for 15 minutes. Meanwhile, beat egg with water in shallow pan. Place flour on sheet of waxed paper. On separate sheet of waxed paper, combine bread crumbs and Parmesan cheese.

Drain eggplant and pat dry with paper towels. Dip in flour, then egg mixture, and finally coat well with bread crumbs, shaking off excess. Place on baking sheet until all slices are coated.

Heat 1/2 inch of vegetable oil in large, heavy skillet over moderate heat. Cook a few slices of eggplant at a time until golden, turning once. Drain on paper towels and serve immediately. Makes 4 servings.

Variation: 2 medium zucchini squash can be substituted for eggplant. Trim ends from zucchini and cut in half crosswise. Then cut unpeeled zucchini into sticks. Do not soak in cold water. Bread in same manner as eggplant and fry until golden. Drain on paper towels and serve.

Eggplant Parmigiana

Tomato Sauce
¼ cup olive oil
1 pound ground round steak
   (or lean ground beef)
1 medium onion, chopped
1 clove garlic, peeled and
   chopped
½ cup celery, chopped
½ cup green pepper,
   chopped
1 (15-ounce) can tomato
   sauce
1 (6-ounce) can tomato paste
1 (16-ounce) can Italian
   plum tomatoes, broken up
   with fork

¾ teaspoon crumbled mixed
   Italian seasoning

Eggplant and Filling
1 medium eggplant
1 egg
2 tablespoons water
Fine dry bread crumbs
½ cup cooking oil
1 cup ricotta cheese
1 (8-ounce) ball mozzarella
   cheese, thinly sliced
½ cup Parmesan cheese,
   freshly grated

Heat oil in heavy skillet. Add ground round, onion, garlic, celery, and green pepper. Cook, stirring, until lightly browned; drain well. Add remaining ingredients and mix well. Bring to boil over moderate heat; reduce heat to low. Cover and simmer 1 hour.

Peel eggplant; cut into 1/4- to 1/2-inch thick slices. Soak in cold, salted water 30 minutes. Drain well and then pat dry with paper towels. Beat egg and water together in shallow plate. Place bread crumbs on sheet of waxed paper. Dip eggplant in egg mixture, then bread crumbs; coat well. Heat oil in heavy skillet. Brown eggplant slices, a few at a time, over moderate heat. Drain on paper towels.

In 13 × 9 × 2-inch casserole dish, place a layer of half of eggplant slices. Dot with half of ricotta. Top with half of mozzarella. Spoon half of sauce mixture evenly over cheese. Repeat layers, ending with tomato sauce. Sprinkle with Parmesan. Bake at 350°F 60 minutes. Makes 8 servings.

Fried Mushrooms

3 dozen mushrooms, about
   1 inch in diameter
2 eggs
1 tablespoon water
½ teaspoon salt

¼ teaspoon pepper
½ cup flour
1 cup Italian-style bread
   crumbs
Oil for frying

Wash, trim stems, and drain mushrooms. Beat egg, water, salt, and pepper together. Impale on a fork and dip in flour, then dip in egg mixture and coat with bread crumbs. Allow to dry while heating 3 inches of vegetable oil to 360°F in a deep-fat fryer or deep saucepan. Fry a few at a time for 4 minutes or until golden brown. Drain and serve hot. Makes 6 servings.

Eggplant Parmigiana

Milanese-Style Rice

½	**small onion, finely minced**
½	**cup long-grain white rice**
1	**tablespoon butter**
1	**tablespoon olive oil**
2	**teaspoons beef marrow**
2	**tablespoons dry white wine**

Pinch of saffron

2	**cups hot beef broth**
1	**tablespoon butter**
2	**tablespoons Parmesan cheese, grated**

Sauté onions and rice in butter and olive oil over moderate heat until very lightly browned. Add beef marrow and cook gently until it melts. Add wine and cook until it is absorbed. Dissolve saffron in hot beef broth.

Add beef broth a little at a time and continue to cook, stirring constantly, until all of the liquid is absorbed and the rice is tender and creamy in consistency. This process should take 18 to 20 minutes. Stir in remaining butter and Parmesan cheese and allow cheese to melt. Serve immediately. This does not reheat well. Makes 4 servings.

Stuffed Zucchini

4	**medium zucchini squash (about ¾ pound each)**
1	**pound ground beef (or ½ pound beef and ½ pound sausage)**
¼	**cup olive oil**
1	**clove garlic, chopped**
1	**medium onion, chopped**
½	**cup green pepper, chopped**
1	**tablespoon parsley, chopped**

½	**teaspoon dried oregano, crumbled**
	Salt and pepper
1	**cup fresh bread crumbs from French or Italian bread**
1¾	**cups tomato sauce (divided)**
¼	**cup Parmesan cheese, grated**

Slice the zucchini in half lengthwise. Scoop out pulp; chop.

Sauté ground beef (and sausage if used) in oil until it loses its pink color. Add garlic, onion, and green pepper; cook 5 minutes. Remove from heat. Add squash pulp, parsley, oregano, salt, pepper, bread crumbs, and 1/4 cup tomato sauce; mix well. Stuff squash shells with mixture. Place in shallow baking dish. Top with remaining tomato sauce. Sprinkle with the cheese. Bake at 350°F 40 minutes. Makes 4 servings.

Venetian Rice and Peas

3	**tablespoons butter or margarine**
¼	**cup onion, chopped**
2	**cups regular-strength chicken broth**
1	**cup raw long-grain rice**

1	**(10-ounce) package frozen green peas**
½	**cup cooked ham, diced**
	Salt and pepper
	Parmesan cheese, grated

In large saucepan, melt butter and sauté onion until transparent. Meanwhile, heat chicken broth to boiling. Add rice to onions and stir to coat with butter. Add peas, ham, and chicken broth and stir well. Cover and cook over low heat approximately 20 minutes or until all of the liquid is absorbed.

Sprinkle with Parmesan cheese and serve. Makes 4 to 6 servings.

Risotto

4	tablespoons butter
1	cup medium-grain or short-grain rice (preferably Italian)
4	tablespoons onion, finely minced

2	tablespoons dry white wine
Pinch of saffron
4	cups hot chicken broth
2	tablespoons Parmesan cheese, grated

Melt 3 tablespoons butter in heavy saucepan. Add rice and onion; sauté until lightly browned, stirring constantly. Add wine; cook until absorbed.

Dissolve saffron in chicken broth. Add broth to rice a little at a time; continue cooking, stirring constantly, until all liquid is absorbed and rice is tender and creamy in consistency. (This should take 18 to 20 minutes.) Add remaining butter and cheese; mix well. Let cheese melt. Serve immediately. Makes 4 servings.

Desserts

Anise Cookies

1 cup butter	3 tablespoons anisette
2 cups sugar	5½ cups flour
6 eggs	1 tablespoon baking powder
4 tablespoons aniseed	2 cups blanched almonds,
1 teaspoon vanilla	chopped

Cream butter until soft. Slowly add sugar; mix well. Beat in eggs, 1 at a time. Add aniseed, vanilla, and anisette; mix well.

Sift flour and baking powder together; stir into egg mixture. Stir in almonds; chill dough 2 to 3 hours.

Lightly grease several cookie sheets. On lightly floured board form dough into flat loaves 1/2 inch thick, 2 inches wide, and as long as cookie sheets. Place several inches apart on cookie sheets. (You should have 6 loaves.) Bake at 375°F 20 minutes. Remove from oven; cool. Slice loaves diagonally into 1/2- to 3/4-inch-thick slices. Lay slices, cut-side-down, close together on cookie sheet. Bake at 375°F 15 minutes, until lightly browned. Cool; store airtight. Makes approximately 100 cookies.

Almond Macaroons

1 (8-ounce) package almond paste
4 egg whites
¾ cup superfine granulated sugar

2 tablespoons cake flour
¼ teaspoon salt

Cut almond paste into small pieces. Work 2 egg whites into almond paste. Slowly add sugar, flour, and salt. Mix well after each addition. Work in remaining egg whites; mix until free of lumps.

Grease and flour cookie sheets. Drop almond paste mixture by 1-inch balls 2 inches apart on cookie sheet. Bake at 300°F 20 to 30 minutes, until lightly browned. Remove from cookie sheet while still warm; cool completely. Makes about 2-1/2 dozen cookies.

Note: Cookies can be decorated with halves of blanched almonds or pieces of candied cherry before baking.

Florentines

½ cup butter
¾ cup sugar
3 eggs
¾ teaspoon almond extract
1 teaspoon orange peel, grated
2½ cups all-purpose flour

1½ teaspoons baking powder
¼ teaspoon salt
1 cup ground almonds
1 cup semisweet chocolate chips
2 tablespoons hot water

Cream butter and sugar. Add eggs 1 at a time, beating well after each addition. Beat in almond extract and orange peel. Sift together flour, baking powder, and salt and add to the creamed mixture; stir well to combine. Add almonds and stir well. Refrigerate dough for several hours. Lightly grease a cookie sheet. Form dough into loaves 1-1/2 inches wide and 1/2 inch thick. Make sure loaves are several inches apart as the cookies spread in baking. Make loaves as long as your cookie sheet allows, but leave at least an inch space between the end of the loaf and the edge of the cookie sheet to prevent burning. Bake at 375°F for 12 to 15 minutes or until lightly browned and a toothpick inserted in the center of the loaf comes out clean. While still warm, cut loaves into 3/4-inch strips and cool on a cake rack.

Melt chocolate chips over hot water, stirring occasionally. When completely melted, stir in just enough boiling water to make a thick mixture with consistency of layer-cake icing. Dip both ends of the cookie strips in the chocolate and allow to dry on a rack until the chocolate has hardened. Makes 3-1/2 to 4 dozen.

Sicilian Iced Cookies

Dough
½ cup margarine
½ cup hydrogenated
   shortening
½ cup sugar
2 eggs
1 teaspoon vanilla
2 cups all-purpose flour
2 teaspoons baking powder
6 tablespoons milk

Icing
2¼ cups confectioners' sugar,
   sifted
3 tablespoons maraschino
   cherry liqueur
A few drops red food coloring
2 tablespoons warm water
Colored candy decorettes

Melt margarine and shortening in a medium saucepan. Remove from heat and add the sugar. Mix well. Beat eggs well and add to the mixture. Add vanilla and mix well. Combine flour and baking powder. Add to butter and sugar mixture and stir well. Slowly add milk and mix to form a stiff dough. Refrigerate dough several hours or overnight. Drop mixture by rounded teaspoons onto a greased cookie sheet. Bake at 350°F for 8 to 10 minutes, or until lightly browned. Cool on a rack.

When cookies have cooled completely, make the icing. Place confectioners' sugar in a small mixing bowl; make a well in the center. Place cherry liqueur and food coloring in the well (use enough to make the frosting a pale pink). Stir sugar into the liquid to form a very stiff paste. Slowly add warm water, while stirring, until mixture is smooth and spreadable. Ice the tops of the cookies and sprinkle with the candy decorettes. Allow to dry on cake racks. Store in an airtight container. Makes 4 dozen.

Crisp Wafer Cookies

½ cup margarine, room
   temperature
⅔ cup sugar
4 eggs, well beaten
1 teaspoon vanilla or anise
   extract

1½ cups flour
1 teaspoon baking powder
Pinch of salt
½ cup nuts, finely chopped
   (optional)

Cream margarine well. Add sugar; beat until light and fluffy. Add eggs and flavoring; beat well. Sift together flour, baking powder, and salt. Slowly add dry ingredients to creamed mixture; mix well after each addition. Fold in nuts. Batter should be soft and sticky.

Lightly grease pizzelle iron; follow manufacturer's directions for baking. Use approximately 1 rounded teaspoon batter for each pizzelle. Discard first 1 or 2 cookies—they absorb excess oil from iron. These cookies keep very well in airtight container or can be frozen. Makes about 3 dozen.

Crisp Wafer Cookies

Neapolitan Torte

Dough

¾ cup butter
1 cup sugar
2 eggs
½ cup ground almonds
1½ teaspoons lemon rind, grated
3½ cups flour

Filling

1⅓ cups raspberry jam (very thick, with lots of fruit)

Glaze and Garnish

2 cups confectioners' sugar, sifted
2 tablespoons hot water
2 tablespoons maraschino cherry liqueur
Few drops red food coloring
½ cup whipping cream
6 candied cherries, halved

Cream butter and sugar well. Beat in eggs 1 at a time. Add almonds and lemon rind; mix. Slowly add flour, mixing in well by hand. Form into large ball; cover. Refrigerate 1 hour. Divide dough into 5 equal parts.

Grease bottom of 10-inch springform pan. Roll out dough 1 part at a time; cut to fit springform pan. Place 1 layer of dough on bottom section of springform pan. Spread with 1/3 cup jam. Top with another layer of dough; spread with jam. Proceed as above until all dough is used. Place ring around springform pan. Bake at 400°F on bottom oven rack 45 minutes. Cool; place on platter.

Mix confectioners' sugar, hot water, maraschino liqueur, and red food coloring to form a smooth glaze. Smooth over top of cake. Whip cream until stiff. Place in pastry bag fitted with rose tip. Pipe 12 rosettes around edge of cake. Top each rosette with 1/2 of a candied cherry. Makes 12 servings.

Crisp Cheesecake

⅔ cup butter
1½ cups flour
6 tablespoons Parmesan cheese, grated
4 tablespoons heavy cream
¼ to ⅓ cup scalded, peeled almonds, cut in half
1 egg

Filling

5 egg yolks
¾ cup heavy cream
⅔ cup butter
½ to ⅔ cup aged cheese, finely grated
1/16 teaspoon cayenne pepper

Garnish
Green and purple grapes

Chop together butter, flour, and Parmesan cheese, either by hand with a chopping knife or in a food processor, using the metal knife attachment. Add cream. Make a dough; divide dough into 2 parts. Make each part into a round, thick cake. Cover them with plastic wrap and refrigerate for an hour or more.

Scald almonds. Peel, and cut them in half.

Separate egg yolks from whites for the filling. (The egg whites are not needed in this recipe but can be saved for several weeks in the refrigerator in a container with tightly fitting lid, or they can be frozen.) Place egg yolks in a saucepan. Beat them together with the cream; let thicken over a double boiler. Stir occasionally with a wooden fork. The yolks should not be allowed to boil. Remove from heat and stir in the butter in dabs. Let each dab of butter totally mix with the egg yolks before adding next dab of butter. Finally, add cheese and cayenne pepper. Let cool.

Remove dough from refrigerator. Roll out dough into plate-size round layers. Roll out between pieces of plastic wrap. Pull away plastic wrap from the top. Place a plate over dough and even off the edges. Turn dough upside down onto baking paper. Remove other piece of plastic wrap. Brush layers with a beaten egg. Garnish one of the crusts with almonds. Bake in a preheated 400°F oven for 10 minutes. Let cool on the paper.

Place the crust without the almonds on a serving plate. It can be moved with the help of the bottom part of a round pan with detachable bottom. Spread cheese filling over the crust. Place almond crust on top. The cake should be made several hours in advance. Garnish it with the grapes.

The layers can be frozen separately. If the cake is put together before it is frozen, it will become soft when thawing and will lose its crispness. Makes 10 servings.

Crisp Cheesecake

Ice-Cream Cake with Chocolate Icing

Ice-Cream Cake with Chocolate Icing

1   quart vanilla ice cream
½ to ⅔ cup walnuts, chopped
2 to 3 tablespoons white rum
    (optional)
4¼ ounces bittersweet
    chocolate

Garnish
**Roasted almonds or pistachio
    nuts**
**Candied violets or silver balls
    (optional)**

Stir ice cream until soft. Add walnuts and rum. Quickly pour mixture into a form with a detachable edge. Place in freezer to harden.

Melt cooking chocolate over a double boiler.

When ice cream has hardened, release the spring on the edge and remove the side of the form. Brush sides and top with a carelessly applied first layer of chocolate. Place ice cream back in freezer without the form edge. Let it freeze again for 1/2 to 1 hour.

Take out of freezer, brush again with chocolate. None of the ice cream should show through after this brushing. It if does, patch up spots with more chocolate. Spread out rest of chocolate with spatula. Sprinkle with the garnish before chocolate hardens. Place again in the freezer.

Remove ice cream from freezer shortly before it is to be served but do not detach it from the bottom of the dish. Makes 6 servings.

Variations: The ice cream is also tasty when about 1/2 tablespoon instant coffee is added. The ice cream cake shown in the picture has been made from doubling the recipe.

Italian Sesame Sticks

1 cup butter or margarine	5 cups self-rising flour
1½ cups sugar	Milk
1 teaspoon vanilla	About 2 cups white sesame
3 eggs	seeds

Cream butter with electric mixer until light. Gradually add sugar, beating well. Add vanilla and eggs, 1 at a time; beat well after each addition. Sift flour. Add to creamed mixture; mix just until smooth. Cover dough. Refrigerate several hours or overnight.

Pour 1 inch milk into shallow pie pan. Sprinkle sesame seeds on large sheet of waxed paper. Using scant tablespoon of dough, roll on board or between palm of hands to 3-1/2-inch long log. Dip in milk, then roll in sesame seeds; coat well. Place on greased cookie sheet 1 inch apart. Bake in preheated 375°F oven 15 minutes. Cool on rack. Makes 6 dozen.

Note: Any leftover seeds can be dried and toasted in the oven and sprinkled on breads or salads.

Fig Cookies

Fig Filling	**Dough**
1 cup dried figs	2½ cups flour
½ cup light raisins	⅓ cup sugar
¼ cup candied cherries	¼ teaspoon baking powder
¼ cup almonds	½ teaspoon salt
¼ cup hot water	½ cup butter
2 tablespoons honey	½ cup milk
	1 egg, beaten
	3 tablespoons butter or
	margarine
	2 tablespoons sugar

First make filling. Put figs, raisins, cherries, and almonds through food grinder, or finely mince. Add water and honey; mix well. Set aside.

Make dough. In mixing bowl, combine flour, sugar, baking powder, and salt. Cut in butter. Beat milk and egg together. Add to flour mixture; mix to form stiff dough. Turn out on lightly floured surface; knead 5 times. Roll to rectangle measuring 18 × 15 inches. Cut into 16 pieces.

Place 1 heaping tablespoon filling in center of each rectangle dough. Fold corners of each rectangle toward center. Place on lightly greased cookie sheet. Brush with melted butter; sprinkle with sugar. Bake at 350°F 20 to 25 minutes, until lightly browned. Makes 16 cookies.

Mocha Cake

Cake
About 1⅔ cups marzipan
2   egg whites from large eggs,
    lightly beaten

Coffee-Cream Filling
About 1⅔ cups heavy cream
Instant coffee, dissolved in a
    very small amount of warm
    water

Garnish
Peeled, thinly slivered
    almonds
1   tablespoon instant coffee,
    dissolved in ½-tablespoon
    warm water
½   cup marzipan
A little whipped cream
Coffee jelly beans/chocolate
    jelly beans

Finely grate marzipan, using a grater. Beat it into a smooth batter with the egg whites. Spread batter out into 3 thin, round "cookies," about 8 inches in diameter, on greased and floured baking-sheet paper. Bake in a 400°F oven for about 10 minutes. Let them cool so that they remain flat.

Whip cream into peaks. Add instant coffee that has been dissolved in a little warm water. It should be very concentrated. Place cakes together with mocha whipped cream between layers, on top, and on the sides. Fasten almonds around the edge.

Mix coffee with the marzipan. Roll it out on baking-sheet paper into a thin round "cookie" the same size as the cake layers. Place it on top of the cake and garnish with a little mocha cream and the coffee/chocolate jelly beans around the edge.

The cake will stay fresh for 2 days, protected by the marzipan. It tastes best when it has been refrigerated several hours or overnight before serving. Makes 8 to 10 servings.

Sweetmeat

1   cup shelled filberts
¾   cup blanched almonds
½   cup flour, sifted
1   cup mixed glacéd fruit
1   tablespoon cinnamon

2   tablespoons mixed candied
    peels, chopped
½   cup sugar
½   cup honey
Confectioners' sugar

Toast filberts in moderate oven; rub in kitchen towel to remove skins. Lightly toast almonds. Combine nuts, flour, glacéd fruit, cinnamon, and candied peels; set aside.

Combine sugar and honey in heavy saucepan. Bring to boil over moderate heat. Reduce heat to low; cook mixture undisturbed to soft-ball stage (238°F on candy thermometer). Pour into large bowl; add fruit and nut mixture; mix well. Place in 2 greased 7-inch-round cake pans (or substitute greased 10-inch pie plate). Bake at 325°F 35 minutes, until firm. Cool; dust with confectioners' sugar. Serve cut in wedges. Makes 12 servings.

Mocha Cake

Bow Knots

1¼ cups flour	½ teaspoon lemon rind
1 tablespoon sugar	2 tablespoons white wine
Pinch of salt	Vegetable oil for frying
1 tablespoon butter	Confectioners' sugar
1 egg	

Combine flour, sugar, and salt in mixing bowl. Cut in butter. Make well in center of flour mixture. Add egg, lemon rind, and wine. Mix to form stiff dough, adding more wine if necessary. Turn out on lightly floured surface; knead until smooth and elastic. Cover; let rest 1 hour.

Roll dough 1/16th inch thick; cut into rectangles 3 × 4-1/2 inches. Make 3 lengthwise cuts in each piece of dough. The strips formed can be intertwined to form knots.

Heat at least 1 inch cooking oil to 365°F; fry 2 at a time until puffed and golden. Drain on paper towels; sprinkle with confectioners' sugar. Makes 15 pastries.

Nougat Ring

Casrata

1½ quarts vanilla ice cream,
    softened
1   quart raspberry sherbet,
    softened
¾   quart pistachio ice cream,
    softened
½   cup candied fruit, diced
2   tablespoons rum

3   large egg whites
½   cup sugar
½   cup whipping cream

Garnish
1   cup whipping cream
Candied fruit

Line 2-quart mold evenly with vanilla ice cream. Freeze until firm, preferably in 0°F freezer. Cover vanilla ice cream evenly with layer of raspberry sherbet; freeze again. Cover with layer of pistachio ice cream; freeze solid.

Cover candied fruit with rum; set aside. Beat egg whites until foamy. Slowly beat in sugar. Whip 1/2 cup whipping cream until stiff. Fold cream and rum-soaked fruit into egg-white meringue until thoroughly combined. Spoon egg-white mixture into center of molded ice cream. Spread to make a smooth bottom layer. Cover; freeze until firm (5 hours, or will keep up to 2 weeks) To unmold, dip outside of mold in hot water 6 seconds; invert onto cold platter.

Whip remaining cup of whipping cream until stiff. Place in pastry bag fitted with decorative tip. Decorate with cream and candied fruit Serve sliced Makes 12 to 16 servings.

Nougat Ring

Cake
2 eggs
¾ cup sugar
¼ cup warm water
¾ cup flour
1 teaspoon baking powder
Bread crumbs

⅔ cup coffee cream
1 teaspoon potato flour
1 cup butter

Nougat
¾ cup sugar
⅓ cup almonds, chopped

Egg-Custard Icing
2 egg yolks
⅓ cup sugar

Beat eggs and sugar together until very light. Add warm water. Sift in flour, which has been mixed with baking powder. Pour batter into a well-greased, 1-1/2-quart, ring-shaped pan, which has been sprinkled with bread crumbs. Bake in preheated 350°F oven for about 40 minutes, or until the cake feels dry. Let cake cool before removing from pan.

To make icing, beat together in a saucepan egg yolks, sugar, cream, and potato flour. Let it come to a boil and become a custard. Remove from heat. Beat until cool. Beat butter until soft and smooth. Beat it into the custard a little at a time.

To make the nougat, melt sugar in frying pan; stir in almonds. Pour mixture onto an oiled baking sheet. Let it cool. Finely chop the nougat.

Divide cake into 2 layers. Spread icing between the layers and around entire cake. Sprinkle nougat over entire cake and press into the icing so that it does not fall off. Refrigerate cake several hours before serving. Makes 8 servings.

Variation: Moisten the cake with a little arrack or rum and water before applying icing. The icing can also be flavored with arrack or rum.

Pears Poached in Red Wine

4 firm ripe pears with stems (about 2 pounds)
1 tablespoon lemon juice
1½ cups rosé wine
¾ cup sugar

1 cinnamon stick
4 cloves
3 strips lemon peel
Lemon slices

Skin, halve, and core pears, leaving stems intact. Place in water with lemon juice to prevent darkening. Combine wine, sugar, cinnamon, cloves, and lemon peel in large skillet. Heat to boiling, stirring to dissolve sugar.

Drain pear halves; add to skillet. Poach over low heat 10 to 15 minutes, until fork-tender (not mushy). Chill (in syrup); serve garnished with lemon slices. Makes 4 servings.

Sicilian Cheese-Filled Pastries

(Cannoli) Pastry
2 cups flour
1 teaspoon salt
2 tablespoons sugar
2 tablespoons soft butter, cut into small pieces
1 egg, beaten
10 tablespoons white wine
Oil for frying
5-inch long × 1-inch in diameter cannoli forms or pieces of dowel

Cheese Filling
⅔ cup sugar
½ cup flour
⅛ teaspoon salt
2 cups scalded milk
2 eggs, lightly beaten
½ teaspoon vanilla extract
¼ teaspoon almond extract
1 pound ricotta cheese
½ cup powdered sugar
½ cup candied fruit, finely chopped
1 (1-ounce) block semisweet chocolate, grated

Prepare pastry. Combine flour and salt in mixing bowl. Make well in center. Add sugar, butter, and egg. Add wine and stir with fork until liquid is absorbed. Turn onto floured board; knead until smooth. Divide dough into 4 equal parts; roll on floured surface until 1/16th inch thick. Cut into 3-1/2-inch squares. Roll squares diagonally onto forms; overlap corners. Seal with a little water.

Heat 3/4 inch oil in heavy skillet to 375°F; fry cannolis, 3 at a time, in hot oil. When light golden, remove from oil. Slip off of forms as soon as cool enough to handle. Let cool completely.

Make filling. Combine sugar, flour, and salt in top of double boiler. Slowly stir in scalded milk; cook over boiling water until mixture thickens. Combine 1 cup of mixture with eggs; beat well. Pour mixture back into double boiler; cook, stirring, 3 minutes. Cool and stir in flavor. (Filling must be cold before adding ricotta.) Beat ricotta and powdered sugar until ricotta is smooth. Fold in custard, fruit, and chocolate. With small spatula, fill cannoli, carefully packing filling. Refrigerate until serving time. Shells can be made ahead, frozen, and filled as needed. Makes 30 to 35.

Wine Custard

6 medium egg yolks
3 tablespoons sugar
1 pinch salt
¼ teaspoon vanilla extract
½ cup Marsala wine

In top of double boiler, beat all ingredients together until foamy. Place top of double boiler over simmering (not boiling) water. Beat constantly with wire whip or eggbeater until mixture becomes thick and hot. Pour into sherbet glass; serve immediately. Makes 4 servings.

Variation: Omit vanilla; add juice and grated rind of 1 lemon.

Sicilian Cheese-Filled Pastries

Frozen Ice-Cream Bombe

1½ quarts vanilla ice cream, softened
1 quart raspberry sherbert, softened
¾ quart pistachio ice cream, softened
½ cup candied fruit, diced
2 tablespoons rum

3 large egg whites
½ cup sugar
½ cup whipping cream

Garnish
1 cup whipping cream
Candied fruit

Line 2-quart mold evenly with vanilla ice cream. Freeze until firm, preferably in 0°F freezer. Cover vanilla ice cream evenly with layer of raspberry sherbert and freeze again. Then cover with a layer of pistachio ice cream and freeze solid.

Cover chopped candied fruit with rum and set aside. Beat egg whites until foamy. Slowly beat in sugar. Whip 1/2 cup of whipping cream until stiff. Fold the cream and rum-soaked fruit into the egg-white meringue, until thoroughly combined. Spoon egg-white mixture into center of the molded ice cream. Spread to make a smooth bottom layer. Cover and freeze until firm (5 hours or will keep up to 2 weeks).

To unmold, dip outside of mold in hot water 6 seconds and invert onto a cold platter. Whip remaining cup of whipping cream until stiff and place in a pastry bag fitted with a decorative tip. Decorate with the cream and candied fruit and serve sliced. Makes 12 to 16 servings.

EQUIVALENT MEASURES

dash = 2 or 3 drops
pinch = amount that can be held
between ends of thumb &
forefinger
1 tablespoon = 3 teaspoons
¼ cup = 4 tablespoons
⅓ cup = 5 tablespoons + 1 teaspoon
½ cup = 8 tablespoons
1 cup = 16 tablespoons
1 pint = 2 cups
1 quart = 4 cups
1 gallon = 4 quarts
1 peck = 8 quarts
1 bushel = 4 pecks
1 pound = 16 ounces

KITCHEN METRIC

measurements you will encounter
most often in recipes are: centimeter
(cm), milliliter (ml), gram (g),
kilogram (kg)

cup equivalents (volume):

¼ cup = 60 ml
⅓ cup = 85 ml
½ cup = 125 ml
⅔ cup = 170 ml
¾ cup = 180 ml
1 cup = 250 ml
1¼ cups = 310 ml
1½ cups = 375 ml
2 cups = 500 ml
3 cups = 750 ml
5 cups = 1250 ml

spoonful equivalents (volume):

⅛ teaspoon = .5 ml
¼ teaspoon = 1.5 ml
½ teaspoon = 3 ml
¾ teaspoon = 4 ml
1 teaspoon = 5 ml
1 tablespoon = 15 ml
2 tablespoons = 30 ml
3 tablespoons = 45 ml

pan sizes (linear & volume):

1 inch = 2.5 cm
8-inch square = 20-cm square
9×13×1½-inch = 20×33×4-cm

10×6×2-inch = 25×15×5-cm
13×9×2-inch = 33×23×5-cm
7½×12×1½-inch = 18×30×4-cm
(above are baking dishes, pans)
9×5×3-inch = 23×13×8-cm
(loaf pan)
10-inch = 25 cm   12-inch = 30-cm
(skillets)
1-quart = 1-liter   2-quart = 2-liter
(baking dishes, by volume)
5- to 6-cup = 1.5-liter
(ring mold)

weight (meat amounts;
can & package sizes):

1	ounce = 28 g	
½	pound = 225 g	
¾	pound = 340 g	
1	pound = 450 g	
1½	pounds = 675 g	
2	pounds = 900 g	
3	pounds = 1.4 kg (in recipes, amounts of meat above 2 pounds will generally be stated in kilograms)	
10	ounces = 280 g (most frozen vegetables)	
10½	ounces = 294 g (most condensed soups)	
15	ounces = 425 g (common can size)	
16	ounces = 450 g (common can size)	
1	pound, 24 ounces = 850 g (can size)	

OVEN TEMPERATURES

275°F = 135°C
300°F = 149°C
325°F = 165°C
350°F = 175°C
375°F = 190°C
400°F = 205°C
425°F = 218°C
450°F = 230°C
500°F = 260°C

Note that Celsius temperatures are
sometimes rounded off to the nearest
reading ending in 0 or 5; the Celsius
thermometer is the same as
Centigrade, a term no longer used.

Index

Recipe photograph page number in italic.